Bhakti and Philosophy

Bhakti and Philosophy

R. Raj Singh

LEXINGTON BOOKS

A division of
ROWMAN & LITTLEFIELD PUBLISHERS, INC.
Lanham • Boulder • New York • Toronto • Plymouth, UK

LEXINGTON BOOKS

A division of Rowman & Littlefield Publishers, Inc.
A wholly owned subsidiary of The Rowman & Littlefield Publishing Group, Inc.
4501 Forbes Boulevard, Suite 200
Lanham, MD 20706

Estover Road
Plymouth PL6 7PY
United Kingdom

British Library Cataloguing in Publication Information Available

Library of Congress Cataloging-in-Publication Data

Singh, R. Raj, 1948-
Bhakti and philosophy / R. Raj Singh.
p. cm.
Includes bibliographical references and index.
ISBN-13: 978-0-7391-1424-7 (cloth : alk. paper)
ISBN-10: 0-7391-1424-7 (cloth : alk. paper)
1. Bhakti. 2. Philosophy. I. Title.

BL1214.32.B53S56 2006
181'.4—dc22 2006017086

Printed in the United States of America

∞™ The paper used in this publication meets the minimum requirements of American National Standard for Information Sciences—Permanence of Paper for Printed Library Materials, ANSI/NISO Z39.48-1992.

To the memory of my Uncle
S. Sukh Raj Singh,
teacher, scholar, patriarch

Contents

Prologue 1

1 Bhakti as a Perennial Concept 7

2 Bhakti and Early Buddhist Thought 23

3 Bhakti and Philosophy in the *Bhagavadgita* 51

4 Bhakti and Love: *Nārada Bhakti Sutra* 75

5 Bhakti and the Philosophies of Art 85

Epilogue 103

Bibliography 107

Index 109

About the Author 113

Prologue

The bond between philosophy and devotion is not hard to surmise. When we take devotion in the larger sense of love, involvement, authentic pursuit, creative activity, a mission, etc., rather than in the narrower sense of religious worship, we understand why the word love (*philia*) abides in the center of the term "philosophy." For what would philosophy be without its devotion to truth and without its devoted practitioners?

In the Eastern tradition of Indian thought a poignant word was coined to represent the love-laden and authentic living of philosophy and the loving experience of religion. That word is "bhakti," usually translated as devotion, and often narrowly understood as "worship." However, a simple etymological analysis and a glance at its historical literary usage, reveals that this term is a synonym of *prema* (love), and its root *bhaj* represents involvement, engagement, participation, pursuit, preference, service, adoration, devotion, and love. All of these attitudes and experiences are basic existential features of the human entity and arise out of basic human aspirations. There is nothing technical or exotic about the activity called bhakti if we explore the various ways the verb *bhaj* was used in ancient Sanskrit literature. However, the term was gradually made more specific, more scholastic, and more narrowly religious by the modern historians and scholars of Indian thought. Its connection with knowledge (*jñāna*), including philosophical knowledge, was rendered obscure in indological scholarship and the bond between bhakti and philosophy was seldom appreciated.

Bhakti is a remarkable feature and tendency of human existence having to do with one's devoted involvement with a person, object, deity, or a creative project. The rich expanse of the tradition of Indian thought reveals a manifold of conceptual as well as lived elucidations of bhakti as part of the various worldviews that emerged from the Indian subcontinent. Even though its first understanding took place in the age of the *Vedas* (2000–500 B.C.), bhakti is usually associated with theism and devotionalism that took Hinduism in its grip after the age of the epics (800–400 B.C.), *Mahābhārata* and *Rāmāyana*, by the modern scholars of indology and religious studies. These scholars also consider the *Bhagavadgita* a watershed in the textual expositions of bhakti, and regard it as the first definitive scripture of Hindu theism. This narrower understanding of bhakti as Hindu devotionalism not only misses the march of bhakti that began with the *Vedas*, but also misses the presence of bhakti in other systems of thought from that part of the world, namely, Buddhism, Jainism, and Sikhism along with other heterodox schools and religious systems. This orthodox view of bhakti set into motion by early indologists overlooks the secular, existential, and philosophical meanings of bhakti as the human urge to love, to belong, and to be creatively involved as part of one's being in the world. Moreover, the philosophical role of bhakti is missed by the early indologists when they understood bhakti as an alternative to *jñāna* (knowledge) rather than the living of *jñāna*.

In addition to offering a philosophical analysis of the relation between philosophy and devotion, which involves a consideration of the connection between knowledge and devotion, this book offers a well-balanced historical account of the conceptualizations and lived experiences of bhakti in the tradition of Indian thought. By well-balanced we mean that our analysis gives due consideration to manifold meanings and interpretations of bhakti, namely, theistic and nontheistic, religious and secular, and religious and philosophical. A history of some standard classical and modern interpretations of bhakti has also been outlined as part of this study.

This book aims to consider the larger meanings and roles of bhakti as it historically emerged in some of the well-known thought systems of India such as Vedānta and Buddhism with special focus on the seminal texts such as the *Vedas*, *Upanishads*, the *Bhagavadgita*, *bhakti Sutras*, and the *Buddhist Sutras*. An objective of this study of the conceptual history of these systems is to specifically trace the connection between bhakti and philosophy as such and the part played by bhakti within the so-called lived philosophies of India. Another conceptual aim of this book is to study the part played by bhakti in the resolution of the enigma of human love, the love between persons as well as the love between the human being and the deity.

The subject matter of bhakti as well as the individual contributions toward its practice and its theoretical elucidations are so vast and its literature so massive, that no single book or even a series of books can lay claim of being comprehensive. Accordingly this short book focuses on some selected but important themes in order to argue for a broader outlook on bhakti than has been offered by the available scholarship. Thus, our historical survey will confine itself to the early period of the emergence of bhakti within the various ancient Indian traditions and shall not delve into the concrete contributions of the saint masters of the later bhakti movements within Hinduism. For although these movements are most fascinating in their largely theistic expressions of bhakti by some of the most outstanding spiritual stalwarts of the Indian tradition, these have already received considerable scholarly attention. What remains mostly unexplored is the earliest, rather secular meaning of bhakti as human love, its role in the development of religions and schools other than those within the fold of Hinduism, and the connection between bhakti and philosophy that lies within the Indian philosophies that are supposed to contain knowledge of reality as well as guidelines to authentic living within them. Bhakti is also visible in the lives and works of Indian religious pioneers and classical thinkers of repute such as the Buddha, the Mahavira, Sankara, Ramanuja, Madhava, and the medieval bhakti saints. It was also the mainstay of modern thinkers such as Vivekananda, Tagore, Sri Aurobindo, and Gandhi.

Indian systems of thought, religions, arts, and literatures remain saturated with the presence of bhakti. They reveal the possibilities of the practice of love and devotion within all fields of human endeavor. However, the larger purpose of the studies of the history of ideas of a specific tradition is not merely to enhance our understanding of that tradition. It is at the same time, a study of the possibilities of human nature and human creativity. It has to be a study of universal human varieties and further reaches of established human preoccupations such as philosophy, religion, art, and literature. Of course, bhakti as a dimension of love is a universal phenomenon. A study of the unfolding of this idea in Indian thought systems reveals something about the possibilities of philosophy as a guide to better living, a philosophy dealing with the real issues of living well, meaningfully, joyfully, and authentically. One expects more from philosophy, than a tedious jugglery of abstract concepts. Its quest for truth does not have to be indifferent to love. As the *Bhagavadgita* says, knowledge and action must be approached with devotion to achieve harmony (*yoga*) in one's living. Thus, our study of the historical understanding of the concept of bhakti in the Indian tradition is at the same time a study of the possibilities of philosophy as such, and of the relation of philosophy with love and devotion. These aspects of philosophy are, for the most part, suggested and occasionally pointed out with brief commentaries rather than explicitly analyzed in the examination of the history of the idea of bhakti that follows.

A more direct aim of this book is to deal with some specific problems of interpretation and some theoretical conundrums with respect to the meaning and the historical evolutions of bhakti on the part of a host of classical and modern scholars. I have provided snapshots of some momentous eruptions of bhakti in the Indian philosophical and religious traditions. In highlighting these moments I hope to illuminate the part played by bhakti in making Indian philosophies and religions what they are.

In chapter 1 a general survey of the historical unfolding of this perennial concept is made over the whole expanse of the tradition. Beginning with the *Vedas* and their appendages, the *Upanishads,* all of the following are briefly appraised with regard to bhakti: the *Bhagavadgita*, the epics *Mahābhārata* and *Rāmāyana*, the great heterodox traditions of Buddhism and Jainism, the religious histories called the *Purānas*, the *Bhakti Sutras*, the southern and the northern bhakti movements, the modern religious tradition of Sikhism. This assessment seeks to point out that bhakti is not just a medieval Hindu phenomenon but was alive and well in the age of the *Vedas*, and in all of the other thought systems and religious traditions of India.

Chapter 2 outlines both the explicit and symbolic presence of bhakti within the grand tradition of Buddhism. It is suggested that an ethos of bhakti was already in place in lands in which the Buddha sojourned and did his ministry. The Buddhist texts including the Pali canon allude to bhakti values and use synonyms of bhakti in their discussions. The chapter deals primarily with early Buddhism, that is, its pre-*Māhayana* phase. *Māhayana*, of course, shows a profound love affair with bhakti, but that food for thought is left for other scholars to delve into. The chapter presents a detailed exposition of the *Mahāparinibbāna Sutta* in order to highlight the aspects of bhakti and other merits of this masterpiece of ancient literature.

Chapter 3 is devoted to an original consideration of bhakti and philosophy in the *Bhagavadgita* which is without doubt an authoritative text on the meaning and value of bhakti. The vital importance of *yoga* (union) of action, bhakti, and knowledge in human life is thoroughly analyzed and recommended in this Song of the Blessed One addressed to the warrior Arjuna. The chapter begins with a critique of the indological scholarship on this seminal text, particularly, its obsessive linkage of bhakti with religious devotion, and its downplaying of the idea of *svā-dharma* (one's vocation, calling), toward which bhakti is also recommended. A new exposition is offered in the last part of the chapter to illustrate the wider functions of the concept and practice of bhakti discussed in the *Bhagavadgita.*

In chapter 4, a philosophical reading of the celebrated bhakti text *Nārada Bhakti Sutra* is offered. It is argued that this composition of one hundred *sutras* (passages) harks back to the original Vedic meaning of bhakti, that is *prema* (love). While it is acknowledged that the bulk of the *sutras* are theistic, nevertheless, a large number of them offer a succinct answer to the age-old philosophical question, "what is love?" The text is interesting for its lucid and concise treatment of the fundamental urge not only to be in love but to understand the phenomenon of love. This text, we argue, not only elucidates the universal issue of the nature of love, but also explains the Eastern standpoint on it.

In chapter 5, the presence of bhakti in the field of art is explored. In particular, a critique of the traditional theories of art within Indian philosophy as well as theories of *rasa* (savor) are examined with respect to their treatment of bhakti. Even though all aspects of Indian art are driven by bhakti, the dominant classical theories of aesthetics did not acknowledge bhakti explicitly either as a *rasa* or as the prime mover of art. The chapter also briefly examines the literary and religious contributions of the bhakti saints of the so-called bhakti movements of Hindu devotionalism. It is shown that despite the plethora of scholarly output on the contributions of these remarkable saint poets, their individual standpoints are not fully appreciated insofar as *nirguṇa bhakti saints* (worshippers of attributeless deity) are lumped together with *saguṇa bhakti saints* (worshippers of specific deities or *avatāras* like Kṛṣṇa). The role of bhakti in the field of art is assessed and briefly outlined in this chapter.

The use of Sanskrit and Pali terms throughout this book has been made in accordance with the original language of the texts in question. While I have provided English translations for all such terms in the beginning of their discussions, I have often used original Sanskrit terms in my own analyses of the issues at hand. The reader is advised to keep the difference between Pali and Sanskrit expressions in mind, especially in case of chapter 2.

It is hoped that these selected expositions of the history of bhakti will show its deep involvement in the thought systems of India as well as provoke thinking about the intimate bond between philosophy and devotion.

1

Bhakti as a Perennial Concept

Bhakti is a remarkable existential tendency that shows itself in the rich expanse of the tradition originating from the *Vedas*. Recognized as a prize possession of the religions, philosophies, and culture of India, it has often won fascination and admiration from students of Eastern heritage. However, its nature, role, and history remain widely misunderstood and have not received all the attention they deserve.[1] Its role as a gatherer of life, love, thought, and the divine is missed in its partial characterizations as "Hindu devotion" or "divine love" or "theism implicit in polytheism." Its status as a perennial thematic concept of the Indian civilization is missed when its pervasiveness is overlooked by the cultural historians preoccupied primarily with its periodic eruptions. Furthermore, the philosophical role of bhakti is eclipsed when it is deemed as an alternative to *jñāna* (knowledge) rather than "the living of *jñāna*."

The aim of this chapter is to reassess the central role of bhakti in an exploration of its nature that is embedded in and provides substance to the historical unfolding of the Indian tradition. It cannot be denied that the idea of bhakti originated in distant antiquity and is present in the earliest hymns of the *Vedas*, and that, in showing itself in various forms and in various periods, it has moved the Eastern mind ever since.

A thoughtful study of the historical expressions of bhakti reveals its existential role. In the following assessment, we will show how bhakti has enabled the existential aspects of life, love, thought, and the divine to abide in the vicinity of each other, and how it has been saving its practitioners from the pitfalls of their distancing from each other. Bhakti was meant to raise the quality of the present existence rather than help in the pursuit of well-defined religious objectives. What the absence of bhakti brings to a lackluster existence essentially aroused dread. At the same time, it is due to their commitment to bhakti that Indian philosophies often earn the name of living philosophies.

The verbal root of the term bhakti lies in Sanskrit "*bhaj*," which means "to share," "to partake," "to resort," and "to participate."[2] Since sharing with persons indicates a communion, "*bhaj*" was used in the sense of love, and with respect to various aspects of love, such as to possess, to enjoy, to prefer, to adore, to worship, to commit oneself, and to be loyal. Bhakti, then, etymologically conveys the sense of participation and sharing. In several classics of Sanskrit literature, composed from the fifth century onward, derivatives of *bhaj* are used to speak about both secular and religious love, including references to the relationship between parents and children, between man and woman, reverence toward a guru, worship of the gods, man's love of God, and God's love of man. The synonyms of bhakti are all synonyms of *prema* (love) such as *priti, sneha, anurāga,* and *anuraki.*[3]

The *Rig Veda*, regarded as the most ancient composition within the body of Sanskrit literature, is an important source of information about the religion and culture of the Vedic Aryan peoples between 2000 and 500 B.C. It contains numerous hymns addressed to several gods, often personifications of the powers of nature or clan gods. If bhakti is an attitude of love, devotion, friendship, and reverence, it is certainly present in these human outpourings of communion with the divine. Homage is paid to, mercy is sought from, and power is recognized of the major gods such as Varuna, Agni, Indra, and several minor deities. Scholars of indology have described man's attempt to measure himself with the divine in the *Rig Veda* as polytheism, pantheism, or "henotheism"—in Max Müller's words, "the belief in individual gods alternately regarded as the highest."[4] Although the term bhakti is not to be found in the *Rig Veda* hymns, the root world *bhaj* is present.[5] The essential tendencies of bhakti, such as recognition of a god's charity, friendliness, and deep involvement in human affairs, as well as man's self-surrendering prayer (*nivedana*), symbolic offerings (*archana*), and sweet recollections of a god's goodness (*smarna*) are all evident.[6] Elements such as wonder, grace, confession, and repentance are there, as is the recognition of the lawfulness of nature in that precursor of the concept of *karma*, the notion of *rta* (moral order). It is noteworthy that in the earliest hymns, the god Varuna is called the controller of the *rta*.[7] The notion of *sraddhā* (faith), the companion concept of bhakti, which is a religious prerequisite of all forms of Hinduism, Buddhism, and Jainism, is certainly present in the hymns, and the term itself is used many times.[8] Nicol Macnicol agrees with scholars like R. G. Blandarkar and E. W. Hopkins, who believe that loving devotion is already present in the *Rig Veda*, when he says: "If we place together into one pattern these fragments of many-hued intuition we may be able to realize how near they approach to the theistic conceptions of today."[9] However, Dhavamony, who is obviously applying the model of later Shaivistic bhakti of South India (beginning in the sixth century A.D.), concludes: "*Rig Vedic* worshipper is yet a seeker of gods, a pious devotee, a friend of gods, god-praising. But this love of god is not at all the later Hindu bhakti."[10]

We must, however, take bhakti in the larger sense, not overlooking its existential roles. What is most interesting is that the devotee of the *Rig Veda* constantly addresses gods as father, mother, brother, relation, and honored guest, and invokes a god's friendship (*sākhya*). This means that religious love was being measured by secular love, or that no distinction was made between *prema* (love) and bhakti. The relation with the divine was one of love and love's attendant expectations, offerings, and involvements. The divine was perceived as dwelling in the vicinity, not far removed either from individuals themselves or from their world. This is indicative of one of the chief roles of bhakti; it personalizes the deity, it does not shy away from authentic anthropomorphism. Life lovingly relates to and holds onto the divine.

For the sake of brevity we must pass over the age of the composition of the *Āraṇayankas* and *Brāhmaṇas*, the appendages to the *Rig* and *Yajur Vedas*, in which bhakti does seem to concede some ground to ritualism, yet manifests itself in the sections devoted to *upāsana* (nearing of oneself to the deity) in the *Āraṇayankas* and especially in the *Satapatha Brāhmana.* The next era, that of the *Upanishads* (700–300 B.C.), is an age of speculation. Here, basic existential questions are spelled out and pursued with a vigor and originality that not only set into motion various philosophical traditions, but resulted in the birth of two great religions, Buddhism and Jainism. The intellectual climate of the times is best described by T. R. V. Murti, who maintains that both the *ātman* (soul) and *anātman* (nonsoul) traditions were in full swing in this age.[11] The nature of the divine, the meaning of life, the worthy objects of thought, the outlining of ethics in consistency with the ontological conclusions, were all being sought after and spelled out. It was in this age that the composition of the epics *Mahābhārata* and *Rāmāyana* had begun. Bhakti blossoms a second time and appears in many forms in the central Vedic tradition as well as in the heterodox traditions of Buddhism and Jainism, performing its existential and ontological roles. The theistic cults of *Pañcharātra* and *Bhāgavatās* were in vogue, resisting the impersonalization of *Brahman* (the absolute) and revealing the splendor of personal devotion to a personal deity. What is remarkable is that bhakti penetrates all speculative and spiritual endeavors of the age.

Along with the attempts to establish ontologies based on the insights of the "know thy *ātman*," we may glean a gradual progression of monotheistic tendencies in the Vedic tradition. In the numerous references to *puruṣa* in the *Rig*

Veda, a concept of supreme reality began to emerge which, by the time of the composition of the *Upanishads*, is recognized as a supreme deity. Vishnu emerges as the dominant god, and his supposed incarnations, *Nārayana* and *Vāsudeva*, the deities of the *Pañcharātra* and the Bhāgavata cults, are adored. We read in *Mahābhārata* that *Shiva*, too, received the highest devotion. Vāsudevism seems to be the largest and most popular religion of the age, for the fourth-century B.C. Greek traveler Megasthenes alludes to the worship of Heracles or Hari, a name for Vāsudeva. There are some inscriptions as old as the second century B.C. set up by devotees of Bhagavān Vāsuveda, most notably one by a certain Heliodoros, a Greek ambassador who describes himself as a *bhāgavata*, or devotee of the *Bhagavān*. Panini, the fifth-century B.C. Sanskrit grammarian also refers to the term *Vāsudevaka,* explained by his second-century B.C. commentator Patanjali as "the follower of the Vāsudeva, the god of gods." The deity Vāsudeva was later amalgamated with that of Krishna.[12] The terms *Bhāgavat* and *Bhagavān,* which share the root *bhaj* with bhakti, were especially reserved for the most superior deities. It is interesting to note that the incarnated Lord that appears in the *Bhagavadgita* as well as the Buddha and Mahavira, were addressed as *Bhagavān* (the Blessed one, the grand dispenser, or *Vibhakta*) by their respective followers.

Thus, we notice that as the Buddha was sharing his existential insight with humankind, as Mahavira was suggesting ways to humans to rid themselves of the mountain of *karma*, and as the philosophical minds were busy with the fundamental questionings, and expositions of the *Upanishads*, the innocent were finding their solace by the way of bhakti. What is remarkable is that bhakti flourished underneath and as part of these three streams and never as an alternative to them. It penetrates them all. It seems that the Buddhists, Jains, and the Upanishadic thinkers had all made up their minds to retain what they regarded as indispensable in the way of bhakti.

The stamp of bhakti in the *Upanishads* is evident in the panorama of their questions concerning the absolute and concerning the actual liberation of man. Bhakti not only enriches the notion of *jñāna*, but also appears as a visible conviction of the Upanishadic seers that a purely intellectual solution to the mystery of Being remains ineffective in securing the goal of actual liberation. The quest for *Brahman* was not a purely metaphysical one, but the pleadings were for liberation from all existential bondage.

> From the unreal [*asat*] lead me to the real [*sat*]
> From darkness lead me to light;
> From death lead me to immortality.[13]

The *Upanishads* contain a rich variety of speculations concerning the absolute and the innermost self of all beings and human beings. The explication of the *Brahman-ātman* equation from manifold points of departure seems to be a central aim of these treatises. However, the relevance of such a pursuit of knowledge (*jñāna*) to life is concomitantly explored, so that knowledge is at once an achievement, a reward, a realization, and authentic living. The futility of metaphysics for the sake of metaphysics is repeatedly exposed and the pitfalls of arid intellectualism outlined. At the same time, the limitations of the endeavors of human intelligence (*prajña*) and the necessity of grace (*prasada*) are recognized. The man-Being relationship is reciprocal, and manipulations of man must cease at some point and await the Being's intimations that appear in thought and instantly have their bearing on life. The following passages from the *Katha Upanishad* say it all:

> This *ātman* is not to be obtained by instruction
> Nor by intellect, nor by much learning
> It is to be obtained only by the one whom It chooses;
> To such a one *ātman* reveals Its own person,
> Not he who has not ceased from bad conduct,
> Not he who is not tranquil, not he who is not composed,
> Not he who is not of peaceful mind
> Can obtain It by intelligence (*prajña*).[14]

These passages seem to echo Socrates's assertion that only the adept in the practice of death, i.e., those who prefer the soul's satisfactions to bodily ones, those who constantly and willingly undergo death of worldliness or body, are true philosophers.

The role of the guru, an accomplished teacher who teaches by the example of his own living, had begun to be recognized in the *Upanishads*:

> Not, when proclaimed by an inferior man is It [*ātman*]
> To be well understood, [though] manifoldly expressed,
> Unless declared by another [i.e., the guru],
> There is no going thither.[15]

One of the functions of bhakti has always been to existentialize metaphysical insights, to translate into the lived world experience an abstract relationship. Holiness is to be recognized as realizable, as evident in the person of the guru. *Guru-bhakti* as well as an explicit theism emerge in the last passage of the *Śvetāśvatara-Upanishad,* the passage that contains the first usage in Vedic literature of the term bhakti in the devotional sense:

> To one who has the bhakti for his god [*devā*]
> And for his teacher [guru] even as for god,
> To him these matters . . . become manifest.[16]

In his commentary, Sankara explains that without the guru's grace, knowledge of the absolute is very rarely possible[17] (*gurukrpa vihaye brahmvidya durlābhati*). Thus, *jñāna* was kept closely allied to life, and the value of a spiritual interpersonal bhakti between the seeker and his guru was acknowledged in the *Upanishads*.

Bhagavad Gita is the first explicit affirmation of theism in Vedic thought. It is at the same time a summary of the insights obtained hitherto by the Vedic and Upanishadic philosophical quest. It fuses into a meaningful synthesis the Vedic cult of sacrifice (*yajña*), the Upanishadic speculation about the *Brahman-ātman* equation, the theism of the Bhāgavata cult, and the *Sāṁkhya* and *Yoga* systems. Bhakti is not only given a new legitimacy, it pervades the whole theistic insight of the *Gita*. Dhavamony informs us that in all the forty-three cases of the usage of the root *bhaj* in the *Gita*, it is nowhere employed in the sense of secular love, sexual or asexual.[18] That means that according to Dhavamony, bhakti in the *Gita* means strictly a relation between man and the *Bhāgavat*. Dhavamony's assertions are subject to debate. In the *Gita*, bhakti in the sense of secular love is implied in terms of Arjuna's friendship with Kṛṣṇa, which evolves into a *guru-ṣiṣya* (teacher-pupil) relationship and then into a man-God relationship.

However, despite this etymological evidence, bhakti in the *Bhagavadgita* continues to build itself on the model of the highest love between persons. Whereas the notion of *avatāra* (incarnation) indicates God's love and care for man's spiritual condition, it is also indicative of the faith that the human form can be the recipient of divinity to the ultimate extent. *Avatāra* is not merely God come hither, it is also guru gone thither. Furthermore, bhakti as human love is evident in the relationship between Arjuna and the *Bhāgavat*, the two interlocutors in the *Gita*. Both allude to *Sāṁkhya* (friendship) between them. The term *ṣhraddhāvān* (faithful) is often applied to a man or woman of conviction and commitment. In chapter 4, the *Bhāgavat* declares: "Verily there exists nothing in this world purifying like knowledge (*na hi jñanena sadṛsam pavitram iha vidyatā*),"[19] and then conjoins, "the man with *sraddhā*, intent on this, with senses restrained, attains this *jñāna* (*ṣraddhāvān labbhate jñānam tat-parah sanyatindriyah*)."[20] *Ṣraddhāvān* are those who, as noted in the *Śvetāśvatara-Upanishad*, have god-like faith in their gurus.

The warm personal devotion summoned by the *Gita* goes hand in hand with the reflective and thoughtful orientations of the Upanishadic insights. Thus the theism that emerges in it remains short of a strict monotheism, which accounts for the fact that the *Gita* will remain a thought-provoking mirror for the Indian mind for centuries to come, and will become a definitive text for all the schools of *Vedānta*, however diverse from each other, as well as for the Vaisanavite and Shavistic religious movements.

In the *Gita*, the significance of the ways of *karma, jñāna,* and bhakti are alternatively explicated with the message that none is to be allowed to captivate us exclusively at the cost of the others. When bhakti is drawn near to *karma*, the age-old problem of the freedom from the law of *karma* (deeds) is resolved. *Karma* is to be performed as if it were an offering to the *Bhāgavat*; the preoccupation with its fruit is to be relinquished in a realization that the best creations are accomplished when they are done for pure creativity's sake. Bhakti must remain allied to *jñāna*, or else knowledge will become divorced from life and there will be confusion as to what is worth knowing. The real knowledge is of course knowledge of the Self:

> Some look upon It [the self] filled with wonder [*ascaryavat*]
> Others speak of It as wonderful [*ascaryavad vadati*]
> Others again hear of It as a wonder [*ascaryavac*]
> Still others, having heard It, do not know it at all.[21]

However, "to the *Brahmin* [scholar] who has known the self, all the *Vedas* are of as much use, as a pool of water is, in the midst of great flooding."[22] It is noteworthy that Arjuna wants to know the human characteristics of the ideal *yogi* whose "intellect is not tossed about by the conflict of opinions"[23] as he pleads the *Bhāgavat*:

> What, O Keshava, is the description of the man
> Of steady wisdom merged in *samadhi* [meditation]?
> How does he speak, this man of steady thought?
> How does he sit? How does he walk?[24]

In response, the *Bhāgavat* not only paints a picture of the man of steady wisdom (*stitha-prajyña*) in the second chapter, but continues to do so throughout the *Gita*. In chapter 16, he describes the characteristics of the men of nondivine (*asura*) nature, who believe that "this world is devoid of truth, it has no moral basis, no god, and no causation other than lust."[25] The attitude toward possessions, interrelationship, and even the food habits of people under the spell of three *gūṇas* (qualities) are identified in chapters 17 and 18. Bhakti clearly appears along with the tendencies to existentialize the metaphysical thought as the needs of the human heart are taken into account in the *Gita*.

When we study the origins of Buddhism and Jainism, we notice that these traditions also embraced the way of bhakti from their very inception. Not only did they inherit the convictions concerning *karma*, rebirth, and the necessity of final liberation from the Vedic tradition, but also the spiritual ethos of bhakti. Bhakti faith that was always the faith of the masses was essentially opposed to the caste system and was characterized by an adoration of the spiritual stalwarts in human form. A proselytizing spirit always pervaded it. The *bhaktās* old and new were never obsessed with their private salvation, but always wanted to share their joyful insights with the masses. Also, the messages of bhakti were always transmitted in the common language, not in Sanskrit. It is likely that all these elements were present in the Bhāgavata and Pañcharātra cults as well as in the social life at the time of the appearance of the Buddha and the Mahavira. They simply adopted all the above-mentioned features of the bhakti ethos in their new systems. After the attainment of enlightenment, the Buddha had no qualms about sharing his *āryasatyas* (noble truths) with humankind. Buddhism and Jainism were both opposed to the caste system, and their founders and saints had a missionary spirit, and spread their word in the common language, at least in the first few centuries. The hierarchies of spiritual status among the *tathāgatas, arhats, jīnas,* and *vīras* (titles indicating spiritual attainment of the saints) within Buddhism and Jainism kept alive a modified *guru-bhakti.*

This is not to say that Jainism and Buddhism do not offer original ontologies. They clearly seem to be reacting to the Vedic assumptions. Buddhism offers an explicitly humanistic and antimetaphysical philosophy. Nonexistential questions were dismissed by it as unfruitful, and the Buddha exercised his majestic silence about theistic speculation, as we read in the *Majjhima Nikāya*, in the so-called arrow sermon of the Buddha:

> The religious life, Malunkyaputta, does not depend on the dogma that the saint exists . . . [or] does not exist after death; . . . whether the dogma obtain that the world is eternal or not eternal, there still remain birth, old age, death, sorrow, lamentation . . . for the extinction of which in the present life I am prescribing. Accordingly, Malunkyputta, bear always in mind what it is that I have not elucidated. I have not elucidated . . . that the world is finite, that the world is infinite . . . that the soul and body are identical . . . that the soul is one thing or body another. . . . And why have I not elucidated this? Because . . . it profits not, nor has to do with fundamentals of religion, nor tends to absence of passion . . . supreme wisdom of Nirvana.[26]

The Buddhists were exhorted to exercise bhakti in the form of *karuṇā* (empathy) not only toward fellow subjects of the *dukkhā* (unsatisfactoriness) of existence, but also toward all beings. The Mahāyana Buddhists elevated the figure of the Buddha to an object of worship, as a personification of the law (*dharma*). The spell of the Vedic gods, especially that of Vishnu, is clearly visible in the historical unfolding of Buddhism. The Buddha's status as a deity and a savior is implicit in the daily prayer of Buddhists, recited to this day: *Buddham ṣarnam gachchami* (I seek refuge in the Buddha).

Indian philosophical and religious authorities and the adherents of various Hindu, Buddhist, and Jain sects were already convinced of the legitimacy, potency, and fascination of the path of bhakti in the first centuries of the Christian era. We learn about the bhakti ethos of this age from the epics and the *Purānas*. Not only was the divine status of Kṛṣṇa and Rama further entrenched, both being recognized as incarnations of Vishnu, but the bhakti of śiva was also in vogue in other circles. The impact of the epics, especially of the careers of their supreme deities, has been so overwhelming that countless poets, dancers, musicians, painters, and sculptors have been enacting and retelling their sagas for centuries. From the sixth century onward, further developments took place in the march of bhakti. The devotional poetic lives and creations of Vaisnavite Alvar and Saivite Nayanar, saints in the south supplied new vigor to theism and heralded what is known as the earlier bhakti movement. In the north, bhāgavatism produced yet another bhakti classic in the form of *Bhāgavata Purāna* in the tenth century.

Vedic insights were turned into systems by some remarkable philosophical minds. Sankara (eighth century), Ramanuja (eleventh and twelfth centuries), Madhava (thirteenth century), and Vallabha (fifteenth and sixteenth centuries) respectively founded the *advaita, vishishtadvaita, dvaita*, and *śuddhadvaita* schools of Vedānta. While these thinkers were primarily preoccupied by the pursuit of *jñāna* (knowledge), none of them de-emphasized bhakti. Even though he was an astute theoretician, Sankara regarded bhakti as a genuine instrument of realizing the Supreme, and he himself wrote hymns and devotional texts. His refusal to be *sanyāsi* (a homeless religious seeker) without his mother's consent, and his insistence on performing her funeral rites, a forbidden activity for *sanyasi*, show a bhakti free of abstractions.

Besides the various treatments of bhakti in the basic texts of the *Vedas, Upanishads*, epics, *Purānas*, and in the works of the philosophers, we also find some works devoted exclusively to bhakti. In these, bhakti is not discussed merely as one of the many paths to spiritual achievement, but its nature is discussed in depth. Among the works of this class, *Śāndilya Bhakti Sutra* and *Nārada Bhakti Sutra* are regarded as the classics. The connection between bhakti and love is succinctly traced in *Nārada Bhakti Sutra*. Believed to be composed around A.D. 1000 by an unknown author, the work consists of eighty-four *sutras*, or aphorisms. This exposition seems to meet the expectation that a philosophy should not only explain things but must explore the possibilities of better living. A detailed analysis of *Nārada Bhakti Sutra*[27] will be given in a subsequent chapter, but let us briefly consider what the *sutra* has to say on the connection between bhakti and love.

At the outset, the first *sutra* promises to explain the doctrine of bhakti and the second asserts that bhakti is indeed of the nature of supreme love (*parama prema-rūpā*). It means that bhakti is called the highest attainment of *prema* (love), and that the *rūpā* (nature) of bhakti and *prema* is the same. The third *sutra* conjoins "also of the nature of immortality" (*amrta-sva-rupacha*). The text provides the insight that the ultimate urge in love is the urge for immortality, i.e., an escape from mortality or from the everydayness or bland ordinariness of human (mortal) existence. The drive in love is one that seeks elevation from the lower existence toward a higher (more fulfilling) existence. The fourth *sutra* says:

> Having gained this [*parama prema*] man becomes
> Accomplished [*siddha*], immortal [*amṛta*], content [*tṛpta*]

The text seems to be saying: this gain of supreme love is a remarkable attainment. It gives one a taste of immortality and yields to one the ultimate satisfaction.

The author further states that this love is not of the nature of lust (*sā nā kāmayamānā*), but rather that a kind of renunciation is a natural result of it (*nirodhrūpatvāt*),[28] for this renunciation is the detachment from all religious and secular commerce.[29] He means to say that the supreme love is not a lustful love but one that finds both ritualism and conventional worldly excitements uninteresting. Next, the *Sutrakāra* considers definitions of bhakti given by other well-known seers, and advises that it should be pursued exactly as described by these divine men, and that the devotee should let bhakti be just as the love of the *gopis* (cowherd women) for Kṛṣṇa (*yathā brajgopikanam*). Such a love is not a love of abstractions, but comparable to the human yet world-renouncing concrete love of the *gopis*.

In *Sutras* 23 and 24, it is said that love without knowledge of the true nature of the beloved is like an illicit love, which is characterized by the absence of happiness-in-the-happiness-given-to-another (*tatsukhsukhitvam*). In other words, in authentic love, knowledge of what the beloved is and what his or her preferences are, is a prerequisite, as his or her happiness becomes one's own. The happiness referred to here is not a matter of giving or receiving or even sharing. One's own happiness lies in and consists of the happiness of the other.

"Because of God's dislike for egoism and because of his love for the meek, bhakti alone is superior to *karma* and *jñāna*."[30] The *Sutrakāra* seems to say that love is what saves one from egoism. Love is not a device to procure satisfaction for the ego, but a moment in which ego is irrelevant. Opportunities of love, or bhakti, remain open for the meek and innocent even as they are open for the haughty and the scholarly. Thus, the path of *parama prema* is preferable to that of *jñāna* and *karma*.

"The nature of *prema* cannot be put into words [*anirvachanīya premas-varūpam*], for it is comparable to the taste enjoyed by the dumb [*muka-asvādana-vat*, i.e., love is indescribable, leaves one speechless], but it is found to manifest itself in some rare deserving recipients of it."[31] Love has the nature of sheer immediate experience (*anubhava-rūpam*).[32] "Just as the being of God is not dependent on any proofs, love is its own proof [*svayam-pra-manatvāt*]."[33] The *Sutrakāra* seems to be saying that love is to be witnessed in the lives of those who have sought it and deservingly found it. It is not to be found in the books of the scholars. Those who possess it do not have to prove it. It shows through their personality; it shows in their life.

Nārada Bhakti Sutra confirms that bhakti essentially is an elevation of "personal love," i.e., it is not a different kind of love. Its rewards are the well-known rewards of *prema* (love). The *sutra* expounds the Indian concept of love based on an overcoming of egoism in a release from the narrower confines of one's superficial self.

The age-old bhakti blossomed into what has been called the bhakti movement, which truly moved the people of India, and placed before them a prospect of poetic living. The period between the thirteenth and seventeenth centuries saw a transformation so great in the religious and cultural life of India that it seemed that a spiritual revolution was under way. The aims of spiritual life shifted toward a passionate and loving preoccupation with one God, called by the names Rama or Kṛṣṇa. Ritualism, scriptural scholarship, meditation by the priesthood, and asceticism were regarded as superficial and unnecessary. Love as bhakti became widely recognized as the soul of all religious, ethical, philosophical, and aesthetic quests. These were also the times that saw the growth of Indian common languages, or vernaculars, as Sanskrit no longer was the first choice of the creative minds. The literature of modern Indian languages was born in the cradle of the bhakti movement, and thus classical literary values remain closely allied with the measures of bhakti. Bhakti saints and gurus emerged in all regions of India, and their amazingly devoted lives and poetic and musical creations won the hearts of millions.

The devotional religion impressed upon the people that the bond with Iśrava (the object of devotion, God) requires nothing but love, and the kindness of Iśrava knows no distinctions of caste, class, or sectarianism. The path of bhakti offered a much-needed strength to a population tired and weakened by oppressive ruling classes, that were often comprised of foreign military adventurers. They were also exploited by a corrupt priesthood, as well as by a firmly entrenched caste system. Bhakti offered dignity, strength, and joy of life to masses in all parts of the subcontinent, as the lovers and bards of the almighty brought the gift of their love songs.

The bhakti movement included an accomplished exponent from Panjab in the person of the Guru Nanak (1469–1539), who founded Sikhism, the fourth major religion originating in India. The guru inspired his *Sikhs* (*Shishyas*, or disciples) to gain union with the almighty through *nāma*, the recalling of God's name in love-laden silent thought.

The work of bhakti holy men is characterized by a very personal and passionate longing to identify with the object of devotion (*Iś*). The role and the superiority of the way of bhakti is very succinctly explicated in the following words of the sixteenth-century bhakti saint Eknath (1548–1608):[34]

> Though one restrains the senses, yet they are not restrained. Though one renounces sexual desires, yet they are not renounced. Again and again they return to torment one. For that reason, *the flame of Hari-bhakti was lit by the Veda.*[35] There is no need to suppress the senses; desire of sensual pleasure ceases of itself. So mighty is the power that lies in *Hari-bhakti*. . . .
>
> The senses that *Yogis* suppress *bhaktas* devote to the worship of *Bhāgavat*, offer to *Bhāgavat*. *Yogis* . . . suffer in the flesh; the followers of bhakti become forever emancipated. Though he has no knowledge of the *Vedas*, still by one so ignorant may the real Self be apprehended. The condition of *Brahman* may be easily attained and possessed. . . .
>
> Women, *Sudras* and all the others . . . can be borne by the power of *Shraddhā* and bhakti to the other bank . . . [of the ocean of *Samsāra* (world)].
>
> Wherever the *bhakta* sets his foot that path is god. Then in every step he takes, his bhakti is an offering to *Brahman*.

According to Eknath, reason's efforts to suppress the instincts were found not only futile but unnecessary by the *bhaktās.* The path of love offers a better life and assured fulfillment. One's lack of scholarship, gender, and caste status were no hindrance in the way of realization (*prāpatti*) of *Brahman.* Eknath affirms that a *bhaktā* is able to know divine immanence "wherever he sets his foot," and every step he takes (everything he does) is "an offering to *Brahman.*" Here is the insight of *Bhagavad Gita* reaffirmed by Eknath, that ethical living is not necessarily the result of ethical programs worked out by reasoning. Ethics without tears, the ethics of love is better than the ethics of exertions. As one recognizes the fundamental object of all one's involvements, that is worth being the origin and goal of one's love and thought, all intentional and oppressive moral interventions are rendered unnecessary.

The march of bhakti continues in contemporary India and the bhakti movement continues, in a way, to this day. People's respect for all claimants of the *bhaktā* status continues, as holy men, *gurus*, *sādhus, swamis,* and *mahatamas* emerge in all regions of the land to interpret the age-old religious concepts for the people in their own diverse languages. The call to shun ritualism and formal sectarianism and to embrace the path of *nāma* and *sevā* (service) is often heard coming from the more authentic of such leaders of people's religion. The method of bhakti continues to be regarded by many as the most potent and delightful.

A look at the history of its manifestations shows us that bhakti has always been the soul of Indian philosophical and religious heritage. It pervades all periods of the cultural history of the subcontinent. Yet, its appearance has been diverse and colorful, sometimes subdued and sometimes passionate. It has worked on behalf of life, love, thought, and the divine, and has demanded from all traditions that all aspects of human existence be gathered together.

Bhakti, we notice, has always advanced the cause of life. The wholeness of existence, its substantiation in death, the life-world situation, and the need to be authentically active and involved, were all exposed by bhakti. How to be liberated from the ills of life, from its harshness, its *dukkhā* (unsatisfactoriness), how to cross over the ocean of *samsāra* (world cycle) were the questions to be dealt with. How can existential concerns be transformed into love's gentle occupation? Bhakti let religion unfold its answer to the love in the human heart and meet the heart's expectations. It let religion be personal religion. Bhakti calls for the familiar instances of *prema* to be transformed into *parama prema.*

Bhakti worked on behalf of thought, for it always saved thought from the stony structures of metaphysics. It pointed toward the pitfalls of quantitative learning, scholarly haughtiness, elitism, and dogmatism, and kept the core philosophical questioning alive. It exhorted thought to remain concerned with its source and be sure about what is worth thinking. The Buddhist meditative practices and the *bhaktas*' preoccupation with *nāma* are all instances of man's attempt to establish a two-way attunement to Freedom and Being in thought.

Bhakti has never let the divine be out of sight. It pointed out the futility of knowing the divine metaphysically. It let the divine retain its unknowableness by attempting to know it through love as far as possible. Bhakti never lets the human-divine involvement be subsumed under formulas such as henotheism, polytheism, monotheism, etc. It does not let the divine be reduced to an object, but invites it to dwell nearby in one's own world. The divine is always received as one's own, for the expectation of own-ness is natural in love.

Thus life, love, thought, and the divine were held closely knit and fused together by the way of bhakti that originated along with the ancient *Vedas*. As a distinct orientation pervading all Indian religions and philosophies, bhakti has always preserved the personal, fascinating, and creative experience.

ENDNOTES

1. M. Dhavamony, in the introduction to his valuable work *Love of God According to Saiva Siddhanta* (London: Oxford University Press, 1971) points toward the poor

treatment of bhakti to date at the hands of indologists and the scholars of religions, both Western and Indian. The role of bhakti remains even more misunderstood due to the fact that it has been narrowly viewed as a merely religious phenomenon. Its larger function as a distinct existential orientation manifesting itself in the philosophical, aesthetic, literary, cultural, and religious life of a historical people has mostly been missed.

2. For a comprehensive etymological and semantic analysis, see Dhavamony, 11–44.

3. Ibid., 20.

4. F. Max Müller, *The Six Systems of Indian Philosophy* (New York: Longmans, 1928), 40.

5. *Rig Veda*, 1–156–3; 8–32–14; 9–113–2, 3; 10–151–2, 3, 7.

6. *Rig Veda*, 5–51–15, 10–151–5, 8–92–19, 8–102–15.

7. *Rig Veda*, 1–25–1, 2.

8. *Rig Veda*, 8–32–14, 9–113–2, 9–113–4, 10–151–2, 3, 7. See K. I. Sheshagiri Rao, *The Concept of Sraddhā* (Patiala: Roy Publishers, 1971), 190.

9. Nicol Macnicol, *Indian Theism* (New Delhi: Munshilal Manoharlal, 1915), 9.

10. Dhavamony, 55.

11. T. R. V. Murty, *The Central Philosophy of Buddhism* (London: Allen and Unwin, 1968), pp. 3–35.

12. R. G. Bhandarkar, *Vaisnavism, Saivism and Minor Religious Systems* (Strasbourg, Germany: K. J. Trubner, 1913), 2–14.

13. *Bṛahdāṛanyaka Upanishad*, 1–3–28. See R. E. Hume's translation, *The Thirteen Principal Upanishads* (London: Oxford University Press, 1921). Hume's translations have been slightly revised for use in this and the following three quotes.

14. *Katha Upanishad*, 2–23.

15. *Kena Upanishad*, 2–28.

16. *Svetāsvatāra Upanishad*, 6–23.

17. *Svetāsvatāra-Upanishad sanuvād sankrabhāsyasahit* (*Svetāsvatāra Upanishad* with the Commentary of Sankara), M. L. Talan, trans. (Gorakhpur, *India*: Gita Press, 1965), 263.

18. Dhavamony, 38.

19. *Bhagavad Gita*, 4–38.

20. Ibid., 4–39, 57.

21. Ibid., 2–29, 34.

22. Ibid., 2–46, 36.

23. Ibid., 2–53, 37.

24. Ibid., 2–54, 37.

25. Ibid., 16–8, 132.

26. *Majjhimanikāya,* H. C. Warren, trans., *Buddhism in Translations* (Cambridge, Mass.: Harvard University Press, 1915), 122.

27. For the complete text and a translation, see *The Sacred Books of the Hindus*, Vol. 7. For a reprint of which see Nandalal Sinha *Bhaktisūtras of Nāradā* (New Delhi: Munshilal Manoharlal, 1998). The texts cited below have been revised by me.

28. *Nāradā Bhakti Sūtra, Sūtra* 7.

29. Ibid., *Sūtra* 8.
30. Ibid., *Sūtra* 25.
31. Ibid., *Sūtras* 51, 52, 53.
32. Ibid., *Sūtra* 54.
33. Ibid., *Sūtra* 59.
34. Quoted by Nicol Macnicol, 270. Translation revised by the author.
35. Italics mine. Eknath clearly seems to be convinced that bhakti originated in the ancient *Vedas* and not with the so-called bhakti movements.

2

Bhakti and Early Buddhist Thought

Bhakti, at a fundamental level, is so essentially a "human" experience, that it cannot be confined to a particular tradition. Since this term is a part of Sanskrit vocabulary and obviously originated and gained currency in certain Vedic religious outlooks and practices, it is often narrowly understood and defined as "Hindu devotion." Thus, expositions of bhakti of a Socrates or bhakti of a Plotinus would be treated as philosophically exotic and culturally hybrid speculations. Even within Indian religious and philosophical traditions bhakti remains narrowly understood both historically and philosophically. It is commonly believed that bhakti suddenly and explicitly appeared with the last couplet of the *Śvetāśvatara-Upanishad* and for the first time enunciated rigorously in the *Bhagavadgita*. It is often narrowly understood as an expression of theism, by many scholars, merely as the *bhakta's* devotion for his or her *bhagvān*, a subject-object relationship, and thus absent in *nāstika* (non-theistic, non-Vedic) religions like Buddhism and Jainism.

However, a simple etymological probe will indicate that bhakti has more anthropocentric and existential connotations rather than being originally and primarily indicative of the human-God relationship. Bhakti was always meant to introduce the human factor into philosophical abstractions and religious enigmas. The role of bhakti as a perennial tendency of Indian thought is missed when its all abiding but subtle presence is overlooked by cultural historians preoccupied primarily with its periodic and spectacular eruptions. The philosophical role of bhakti is missed when it is viewed as an alternative to *jñāna* (knowledge) rather than "the living of *jñāna*." A succinct meaning of bhakti, as pin-pointed by a later classic *Nārada Bhakti Sutra* (tenth century) is *parama prema* (higher attainment of love). As "loving devotion" and a basic involvement of the human soul with things it finds valuable and fulfilling, bhakti is not a sole possession of Indian philosophies and religions. As a basic longing of human heart and as a basic existential feature, it is universal. However, Indian traditions offer a remarkable fusion of bhakti and *jñāna,* as well as some rigourous investigations into and experimentations with the nature of bhakti. A study of Indian worldviews from the pivotal point of bhakti reveals original and fascinating insights into human nature and human potential.

The aim of this chapter is to show that bhakti was already in vogue in religious circles when the Buddha appeared on the Indian religious scene. This ancient form of bhakti was not only a catalyst in the formation of the Buddha's new worldview, but bhakti continues to pervade the *dharma* of the Buddha in its early doctrinal period as well as in its *Mahāyana* developments. In order to identify the pervasive but subtle presence of bhakti in the earliest statements of the Buddha *dharma*, both bhakti and *dharma* need to be precisely defined in terms of their essential as well as relevant philosophical meanings and implications. This means that we will retrace the broader and original meaning of bhakti in order to study its role in the formation and elucidation of the Buddha's *dharma*. However, as we shall see *dharma* carries several special meanings within Buddhism, and thus in this short chapter we cannot possibly enumerate all the various ways of bhakti that are visible in Buddhist ethics, religious practices, movements, and doctrinal developments. Thus, we will confine ourselves to Buddha-*dharma* in the sense of "the basic teachings of the Buddha" and will remain focused on the pre-*Mahāyana* period. When we glean through the records of early Buddhism, we notice that even though the ancient Buddhist *sutras* do not show any debt to the *Bhagavadgita* and did not produce bhakti classics such as the *Bhāgavat Purāna, Nārada Bhakti Sutra,* and *Śāndiliya Bhakti Sutra,* bhakti not only shaped the existential focus of Buddhism but remained part and parcel of that tradition. Nicol Macnicol in his *Indian Theism* published in 1915, has a chapter titled "Theism within Buddhism" which gives an account of the presence of bhakti within early and *Mahāyana* Buddhism.[1] More recently B. G. Gokhale (1981) has explored the aspects of bhakti in the first five centuries of Buddhism in his article "Bhakti in Early Buddhism."[2] Both of these scholars have contributed toward correcting the view that bhakti is exclusively a Hindu practice and have shown with attention to detail the presence of bhakti in Buddhism with citations from *Nikāyas* and *Mahāyana* documents. However, Macnicol is obviously equating bhakti with theism, and Gokhale is too sure about the meaning of bhakti as faith (*śradhā*). Says Gokhale,

> There is no need for us to go into the detailed implications of the philosophical aspects of the history of faith and knowledge since we are concerned here with the development of the bhakti element in early Buddhism. . . . Nor is there much need for us to discuss at length the origin and development of the term bhakti in Brahmanical literature, [or] . . . whether the movement . . . originated first . . . in its Vāsudeva-Kṛṣṇa evolutions.

In my view, however, the philosophical implications of the idea of bhakti, an understanding of its etymology, and an appreciation of its history are of utmost importance. One has to have a picture of "the thought ferment" of the sixth- and fifth-centuries B.C. India to study the continuing presence of bhakti in the Buddhist outlook. Not only *karma* and rebirth but also bhakti constitute what Buddhism shares with Vedānta. Furthermore, one can only "attempt" to define perennial thematic concepts such as bhakti. These are never conclusively or exhaustively defined, for to do so will be an oversimplification. Thus, to study the rise of bhakti in Buddhism we will proceed toward the times of the Buddha by way of a short historical overview of the pre-Buddhist evolution of bhakti and its presence in the non-Buddhist and non-Jaina schools and sects of the age in which the Buddha put forward his worldview.

But before we do so, a brief note on the various chief meanings of *dharma* within Buddhism is in order. The word *dharma* carries various meaning in the early Vedic as well as in early Buddhist traditions. Needless to say it cannot be defined easily nor can it be translated casually. The law or lawfulness, the ground, the established order, the moral order, duty, doctrine, religion, the fundamental nature of things, etc., are some of its traditional meanings. It is a word that was well chosen by the Buddha for the body of his doctrine and for his new heterodox religious system as a whole. It is well known that the term *dharma* has been widely employed within Buddhism in three significant ways. Firstly *dharma* is understood in the sense of "Buddha-*dharma*" that is the teaching or the body of the doctrine of the Buddha. As indicated in the triple refuges sought by the Buddhists in their daily prayer, namely, the refuge in the Buddha, in the *dharma*, and in the *sangha* (the order), the truth of the teaching is to be viewed as independent from the personality of the teacher. That the Buddha wished the noble truths to take precedence over himself and the doctrine itself to remain the true and everlasting teacher of the *sangha* is testified by the various extant records (*sūtras*) of his discourses and made abundantly clear in *Mahāparinibbāna Sutta*, which reports on the last moments of the life of the Sakyamuni Buddha. This *sūtra* is comparable in many ways to Plato's *Phaedo* insofar as it succinctly recapitulates the personal standpoints of the master, his entire life's philosophy in one last session of death contemplation. That the *dharma* or the truth is one thing and the authority of the Buddha another is clearly stated in this oft-quoted concise passage from the *Anguttara Nikāya*:

> Whether the Buddhas arise, O *bikhus*, or whether the Buddhas do not arise it remains a fact and the fixed and necessary constitution of being, that all its constituents are transitory, . . . *dukkhā* . . . (and) lacking in *attā*. This fact a Buddha discovers and masters, and when he has discovered and mastered it, he announces, teaches and publishes, proclaims, discloses, minutely explains and makes it clear, that all the constituents of Being are transitory . . . *dukkhā* . . . (and) lacking in *attā*.[3]

The second broad sense in which the term *dharma* is employed within Buddhism is that of proper conduct, moral conduct and duty. Due to the prevalence of the bhakti ethos, this proper conduct was meant to have nothing to do with the traditions of *varña dharma* (duties of the caste to which one belongs), but it means moderate and fitting conduct indicated by the term *samma* in the fourth noble truth. It may also mean code of conduct prescribed for the *bhikkhus* (monks) and *upāsakas* (novices). The third important use of the term *dharma* within Buddhism is *dharma* as reality or "the way it is." *Dharma* is not only understood as reality and as the nature of things but "realities" are also called *dharmas*. We should keep in mind that "reality" is understood in its dynamic and transitory sense and *dharmas* are not taken as substances but as irreducible ultimates.

Besides these three chief uses of the term *dharma* several of its other ontological and cosmological meanings are traced within Buddhism in general and Buddhist philosophical schools in particular. However, in the following study of the bond between bhakti and the Buddha-*dharma*, we will confine ourselves to *dharma* in the first above-mentioned sense. Let us turn now toward the original and ancient meaning of the word bhakti.

As indicated in chapter 1, the verbal root of the term bhakti lies in Sanskrit *bhaj*, which means "to share," "to partake," "to participate."[4] *Bhaj* was used in the sense of love, and with respect to various tendencies and implications of love, such as to possess, to enjoy, to prefer, to adore, to worship, to commit oneself, and to be loyal. Thus, bhakti has the basic sense of involvement, participation, and sharing. In the classics of Sanskrit literature composed from the fifth century onward, derivates of *bhaj* are used to speak about both secular and religious love, about the relationship between man and woman, about reverence toward a guru, worship of gods, man's love of god, god's love of man. The synonyms of bhakti are all the various shades or even types of love such as *priti, sneha, anuraga, anurāki*, etc.[5]

The emergence of bhakti as a concept and as the authenticity of relationships is certainly described in various parts of the *Vedas*. *Rig Veda* contains numerous hymns to several gods, often personifications of the powers of nature or clan gods. Bhakti as an attitude of love, devotion, friendship, and reverence, is certainly present in these hymns indicative of an innocent human relationship to the divine. In these records of divine adoration and wonder, major gods, such as Varuna, Agni, Indra, and several minor deities are worshipped. Although the term bhakti is not to be found in the *Rig Veda* hymns, the root word *bhaj* is present.[6] The various forms of bhakti such as recognition of a god's involvement in human affairs, prayer (*nivedana*), symbolic offering (*arcana*), and sweet recollections (*smarna*) are all evident. The notion of *śradhā* (faith) the companion concept of bhakti, which will become a religious prerequisite of all forms of Hinduism, Buddhism, and Jainism is certainly present in these hymns, and the term itself is used many times.[7]

What is most interesting is that in the antiquity of the religious life of India the devotee of the *Rig Veda* constantly addressed gods as father, mother, brother, relation, and honored guest and appealed to god's friendship (*sākhya*). This means that religious devotion was modeled on the more familiar experiences of secular love; that is, no sophisticated distinction was made between *prema* and bhakti. The relation with the divine was one of love and love's usual expectations and demands. It was an innocently demanding love. This love appears in the sense of *karuṇā* within Buddhism as *guru-bhakti* for the Buddha is also quite visible in the *sutras*.

BHAKTI IN THE TIMES OF THE BUDDHA

The age of the classical *Upanishads*, is one of philosophical speculation and religious innovation. In these times, basic existential questions are raised and pursued with a vigor and originality that not only set into motion various philosophical traditions, but resulted in the birth of various heterodox schools, including Buddhism and Jainism. It was later in this age that the epics *Mahābhārata* and *Rāmāyana* were composed. Thus, bhakti blossoms a second time and appears reinvigorated in the folklore of the epics and in many other forms in the central Vedic tradition as well as in the heterodox traditions of Buddhism and Jainism. There is concrete historical evidence that theistic cults of Pañchāratra and Bhāgavatas were in vogue, which may be called the first concretizations of theistic bhakti.[8] These cults resisted the impersonalization of *Parabrahman* (ultimate absolute) of the *Upanishads*. What is remarkable is that bhakti penetrates all speculative and religious traditions of the age: the Upanishadic thought, Jainism, Buddhism, as well as the Bhagavata and Pañcharātra faiths. The culture of bhakti pervades even the sects called *nāstikas*, that is, those who did not recognize *Vedas* and their appendages as the supreme authority. These sects such as *Jatilas*, *Charvakas*, and *Ajivikas* have not left any written scriptures or documents of their own, but are referred to in the *Vedas*, *Brahmanas*, *Araṇyakas*, and *Upanishads* (Vedic texts), both derogatorily and in terms appreciative of their asceticism, religious drive and spiritual quests. However, almost all references to them in the Buddhist and Jain *suttas* are critical and unappreciative. For instance in *Brahmajāla sutta* of the *Dīgha Nikāya*, sixty-two non-Buddhist schools are mentioned and are said to hold wrong views or *michchhaditthi*. The *Śrmanas* and *Jatilas*, who did not recognize the *Vedas*, are mentioned in many ancient texts. Buddhism and Jainism were themselves *śramana* sects. The *Vināya* mentions Alara Kalama and Uddaka Ramaputta with whom the Buddha had personal contact. Some of the religious leaders called *titthiyatirathkāra* or heretics in ancient Buddhist *sūtras* were: Purāna Kassapa, Pakudha Kacayana, Makkhali Gosala, Ajita Kesakamblin, and Sanjya Belathiputta. One of the surviving sects was that of the *Ajivikas* which lasted up to the fourteenth century A.D.[9] Although the *Ajivikas, Cārvākas,* and other prominent *nāstika* sects were the target of Buddhists, Jains, and the *āstika (believers in the Vedas)* faiths, the *nāstikas* also participated in a common religious ethos. A culture of *guru-bhakti* was already in vogue by the time the Buddha and Mahavira appeared. The *Rig Vedic* tendency to anthropomorphize religious devotion reflects itself in the *guru-bhakti* upheld in *Śvetāśvatara-Upanishad.*

This tendency of bhakti attitude to uplift *prema* to *parama prema*, begins to perceive the presence of godliness in the person of the guru. This belief is fully in evidence in early Buddhism. It is interesting to notice that the incarnated lord that appears in the *Bhagavadgita*, as well as the Buddha, Mahavira, and the deities of the *Bhāgvata* faith were addressed as *Bhagvān*, a term applied to the supreme object of bhakti.

Since Buddhism and Jainism appeared at a time when the ethos of bhakti was already established, these traditions embraced a concept of *dharma* as well as *guru-şişya* relationship, which was common among all religious traditions of the times. The beliefs concerning *karma*, rebirth, and the necessity of final liberation were upheld, albeit modified to accord with their respective standpoints. Bhakti faith that was always the faith of the masses was essentially opposed to the caste system and was characterized by an adoration of the spiritual masters in human form. These spiritual masters, who led exemplary lives, were never obsessed with their private salvation, but always wanted to share their joyful insights with the masses. The religious experiences and messages of these saints were always transmitted in the people's languages and not in the languages of the priests such as Sanskrit. All these practices were present in the Bhāgavata and Pañcharatrā cults as well as social life at the time of the appearance of the Buddha and the Mahavira. They simply adopted all the above-mentioned features of the bhakti faith in their new systems. After the attainment of enlightenment, it was natural for the Buddha to wish to share his *arya-satyas* (noble truths) with humanity. Buddhism was opposed to the caste system, and its founders and saints had a missionary spirit, and spread their word in the common languages, at least in the first few centuries. Historians point out that Buddhism appeared in the times of a social upheaval. The agrarian society and dominance of the priestly (*brahmin*) caste underwent a significant change. With the rise of the monarchical and oligarchical states, the *kştriyas* (warriors) and *vaiśyas* (mercantile) classes became more dominant as large cities developed around trade activities. However, the hierarchies of spiritual status among the *tathāgatas, arhats,* and *bhikkhus* within Buddhism kept alive a modified *guru-bhakti*. This is not to say that Buddhism does not offer an original ontology or a new way of life. It clearly reacts to the Vedic assumptions. Buddhism offers an explicitly ethical, humanistic, and anti-metaphysical philosophy. Non-existential and merely metaphysical questions were dismissed by it as unfruitful, and the Buddha exercised his majestic silence about theistic speculation, as mentioned in the *Majjhima Nikāya*, in the so-called arrow sermon of the Buddha.[10] Buddhism shows the same preoccupation with existential questions and nonmetaphysical orientations that were typical of the bhakti ethos, namely, regard for the spiritual masters (*arhats*), opposition to the caste system, imparting of religious teachings in the people's languages and a focus on existential issues.

Thus bhakti as the practice of love, as the existential rather than metaphysical approach, as the fusion of the abstract truth with ideal ways of living, the doctrine (*dharma*) and its abiding presence in its adept practitioners (*arhats*) comes into and pervades Buddhism well before the arrival of *Mahāyana*. It is this ancient form of bhakti that makes Buddhism a living philosophy as well as a philosophical religion. In the *dharma* of the Buddha, the fusion between *nirguṇa* (abstract, attributeless) and *saguṇa* (concrete with attributes) bhakti takes place. It is visible in the Buddha's last words recorded in the *Mahāparinibbāna Sutta*: "decay is inherent in all component things, work out (your *nibbāna*) with diligence." Abstract truth is offered here as an impetus for *the* ultimate project of existence. This fusion between *nirguṇa* and *saguṇa* is visible, as Vinoba Bhave explains, in the daily prayer of the Buddhists, seeking refuge in the Buddha (*saguṇa*) and in the *dharma* (*nirguṇa*) and in the *sangha*-community (*saguṇa*).[11] This *saguṇa* bhakti shows through the logical analyses of the implications of dependent origination in Nagarjuna's *Mūlamadhyamīka-kārikas*. In his works, Nagarjuna does not lose sight of the existential issues at hand and shows his care for the *saguṇa* as he intersperses his discourses with tributes to his master. The following are some examples from his *kārika*:[12]

> In the admonition to Katayana, the two theories concerning "existence" and "non-existence" have been refuted by the bhagvān who is adept in existence as well as non-existence. (XIV–7)
>
> The great sage (*mahā munih*) has stated . . . that *samsāra* is without beginning and end. (XI–1)
>
> The supreme ascetic has said action is volition as well as volitional. (XVII–2)
>
> Such it is reminisced, is the immortal message of the Buddhas, the patrons of the world (*lokānathānam*). (XVIII–11)
>
> I reverently bow to Gautama who, out of compassion, has taught the true doctrine in order to relinquish all vices. (XXVII–30)

BHAKTI ETHOS IN THE EARLY *SUTRAS*

If bhakti is a suffusion of human love with religious love (*parama prema*) or an induction of the human model of love into religious intuition or an uplifting of human love to the level of religious love, then bhakti certainly cannot be confined to theistic Hinduism. As the soul of Vedic religious ethos, it was present in all ancient sects *Āstika* (orthodox Vedic) and *Nāstika* (heterodox or non-Vedic) alike. Unique resolutions of basic human predicaments and religious decorum of *guru-bhakti* were present in all *Nāstika* religio-philosophical schools such as *Cārvākas*, *Ajivikas*, *Jatilas*, etc., as well as in the new religions of Buddhism and Jainism. The quest for the resolution of existential enigmas and the deepest respect for the spiritual masters crossed over sectarian boundaries. When the historical Buddha appeared on the sub-continent of India, bhakti was fully in vogue.

Dwelling in the land of bhakti, the Buddha acted according to the decorum of bhakti and adopted its parameters, that is, those of a living philosophy, in his thought system. The *nirguṇa-bhakti* in the *dharma* of early Buddhism is harder to glean than the *saguṇa-bhakti* of *Mahāyana*, nevertheless an attempt should be made to trace the manifold aspects of the wider notion of bhakti in the foundations of Buddhism.

> Looking over the four continents with their attendant isles, he reflected: In three of the continents the Buddhas are never born; only on the continent of India are they born.[13]

In the early, that is, pre-Māhayana *sūtras*, bhakti appears as the religious ethos and as the remarkably existential approach taken by the Buddha. This approach represents a concern for the good life and the destiny of the human entity, self-reliance on the part of the individual and the rejection of the metaphysical and the abstract.

Let us first consider how bhakti penetrates the religious ethos of the times. The style of reporting the teachings of the Buddha within the early *sūtras* shows how reverently the Buddha was treated by the monks, the general populace and on occasion royal persons. He was addressed as *Bhagavān* or the Blessed one, a title reserved for the incarnations of God, such as kṛṣṇa. There was an etiquette in place for all visitors seeking his audience. Here is a *sutra* from the *Samyutta Nikāya* indicative of the typical reverence and decorum of bhakti toward the Buddha:

> Thus have I heard
> on a certain occasion the Bhagvan was dwelling at Savatthi
> in Jetavana monastery in Ananthapindika's Park.

> Then drew near a certain *bhikkhu* (monk) to where the Bhagvan was, and having drawn near and greeted the Bhagvan he sat down respectfully at one side. And seated respectfully at one side the *bhikkhu* spoke to the Bhagvan, as follows:
> Pray Reverend Sir (*bhante*), let the Bhagvan teach me the *Dharma* in brief. . .
> Then the *bhikkhu* applauded the speech of the Bhagvan and returned thanks, rose from his seat, and saluting the Bhagvan and keeping his right side towards him, he departed.[14]

The *sutra* goes on to describe the rewards of devotion and saintly life in a typical phraseology:

> Then the *bhikkhu*, solitary, retired, vigilant, strenuous and earnest, in no long time, and in his lifetime came to learn for himself, realize and live in the possession of that highest good to which the holy life conducts, and for the sake of which youths of good family so nobly retire from the household life to the houseless one. And he became conscious that rebirth was exhausted, that he had lived the holy life, that he had done what it behooved him to do, and that he was no more for this *samsāra*.[15]

The scriptures of Hinduism, Buddhism, and Jainism, including the epics and legendary histories as well as the secular literary works of ancient India reveal that a culture of bhakti was in place in those times. *Guru-bhakti* in the sense of the highest regard for the spiritual masters of all persuasions, patronage of the saints and *şrmanas* (ascetics) of various sects by the general populace in the form of donations and care of their physical well-being and material needs was widely and indiscriminately practiced. The royal patronage for the ancient and new faiths is well documented in the history of ancient India. The kings freely and voluntarily accepted the higher status and authority of the religious masters and ascetics and paid homage to them. Often the royal patronage was extended to all sorts of sects, as in the case of Emperor Asoka who converted to Buddhism in the third century B.C. It is curious that a sort of *guru-bhakti* and a *guru-şişya* (guru-disciple) relationship existed even among the *Nāstika* (nonbelievers) sects such as the *Ajivikas* and *Cārvākas*. *Ajivikas* were a sect of ascetics who believed in the strict determinism of destiny (*niyati*) and posited no deity or creator, nevertheless practiced *guru-bhakti*. The movement lasted from sixth century B.C. to the fourteenth century A.D. *Cārvākas* were the materialists, whose legendary *Brhaspati Sutra* also dates back to 600 B.C. *Cārvākas* are often derogatorily mentioned in the *Mahābhārata*, *Visṇu Purāna*, and the Laws of Manu as well as in the Buddhist and Jain *sutras*, and their materialistic doctrines are briefly described in the *Sarvasiddhānta-samgraha* of Sankara and the *Sarvadarsāna-samgraha* of

Madhava. The ancient drama *Prabodha-Candrodaya*, indicates that a *guru-bhakti* was in place even in the atheistic and materialistic school of *Cārvāka*. In the drama, a character called Passion applauds and elucidates the doctrine of Vacaspati or Brhaspati as follows:

> The *sastra* (scripture) whose doctrines are obvious to all, and which is founded on the evidence of the senses, which admits only the elements of earth, water, fire, air; which maintains that sustenance and love are the objects of human existence; which asserts that matter possesses intelligence; which denies the existence of separate spirits, and affirms that death is blessedness, was written by Vachaspati, a believer in this system; he delivered it to a *Cārvāka*, who taught it to his disciples and these disciples instructed their followers. Thus it has become widely diffused in the world.[16]

The following may be a mockery of the religious speak but this is how the *Cārvāka*, the character in drama responds:

> By your bounty all are happy. Having accomplished what he (Kali, the spirit of so-called sinful age, i.e., *kaliyuga*) was ordered to perform, he now desires to touch your feet; for blessed is he who after destroying the enemies of his Lord beholds his gracious face with exceeding joy, and prostrates himself at his lotus feet.[17]

The spirit of bhakti pervaded the religious ethos in ancient India and continues to sustain the religious life of modern India. This is bhakti in the larger sense that appears in the form of deference given to the religious stalwarts, and in the use of religio-philosophical concepts as guidelines for better living. It is evident in the more reverence given to the philosopher than to philosophy, in letting the abstract subserve the existential, in the focus on the woe and weal of the human. All these elements of the wider sense of bhakti were carefully adopted, cultivated, refined, and reinstituted by the Buddha. The formation of the *Sangha*, the necessity of taking refuge in the *Sangha*, adherence to the rules of discipline (*vinaya*), the hierarchies of religious accomplishments, the difference of status between lay persons, junior monks, and senior monks, all those measures taken by the Buddha and by the early Buddhists were geared in a way toward the institutionalization of bhakti within the fold of the new faith. Out of the three major divisions or baskets (*pitakas*) of the Buddhist canon, the first is named the *Vināya-pitaka* (the Discipline-Basket), the second contains the discourses or *sutras* and is called the *Sutra-pitaka*. The third is composed of commentaries on the *sutras* and called *Abhidharma-pitaka*. This three-fold division of the Buddhist scriptures indicates that philosophical discourses and their scholarly analyses were not deemed adequate, even though Buddhism offers one of the most original and outstanding philosophical accounts of human existence. The *Vināya* or disciplined living of *dharma* was deemed most essential. It is as if the *yoga* of *jñāna* and *bhakti* with *karma* as advised in the *Bhagavadgita* was perceived as vitally important in another way by the Buddha.

People's adoration of the Buddha and the Buddha's love of humanity is graphically described in an account of the Buddha's daily habits in *Sumangala-Vilasini* (1–45–10) as part of Buddhaghosa's commentary on the *Dīgha Nikāya*:

> By these tokens the people would know "the Blessed One has now entered for alms," and in their best tunics and best robes with perfumes, flowers, and other offerings, they issue forth from their houses into the street. Then, having zealously paid homage to the Blessed One with perfumes, flowers and other offerings, and done him obeisance, some would implore him "Reverend Sir, give us ten priests to feed," some "give us twenty" . . . and they would take the bowl of the Blessed One and prepare a seat for him, and zealously show their reverence by placing food in the bowl. . . .
>
> When he had finished his meal, the Blessed One, with due consideration for the different dispositions of their minds, would so teach them the *Dharma*. . . .[18]

The Buddha, like Socrates and Jesus wrote nothing, but preferred to appeal directly to the hearts of the people; it was through the practice of love (bhakti) that his message would endure. He spelled out the *dharma* for his audiences throughout almost forty-five years of his ministry "with due consideration for the different dispositions of their minds" as the above *sutra* informs us. He spoke the language of the people and not the language of the scholars, *Magadhi* or *Pāli* rather than Sanskrit. As the title of the *sutra* containing his first sermon concerning the four noble truths indicates, he carried out a *dharma chakra parivartana* (turning of the wheel of *dharma*) or a radical transformation of the content of *dharma* from the abstract to the concrete, from the metaphysical to the existential, from *tarka- jñāna* (abstract knowledge) to bhakti-*jñāna* (knowledge through love), as he put his finger on the real problem of human existence, namely, the problem of *dukkhā* (pain; unsatisfactoriness) in the first noble truth:

> Now this, O *Bhikkhus* is the Aryan truth of *dukkhā*; birth is *dukkhā*, decay is *dukkhā*, disease is *dukkhā*, death is *dukkhā*. Union with the unpleasant is *dukkhā; dukkhā* is the separation from the pleasant; and any craving that is unsatisfied, that too is *dukkhā*. In brief, the five aggregates (*skandhās*) that spring from attachment are *dukkhā* .[19]

The empathy (*karuṇā*) with the inevitable sufferings of human condition, to prepare humans to encounter inevitable change and to elucidate anew the path to salvation (nirvana) were the main concerns of the Buddha *dharma*. The practice of love is part and parcel of this kind of humanism. Bhakti penetrates this humanism. Bhakti is definitely involved in this analysis and program of life and living. The Buddha seems to have incorporated both the fundamental as well as the formal aspects of bhakti in his *dharma*. In the *Mahāparinibbāna Sutta*, which describes the events leading up to his death, the Buddha is shown as ensuring that the spirit and practice of *bhakti* will survive.

> It may be Ananda, that some of you will think "the word of the Teacher is a thing of the past; we have now no Teacher." But that, Ananda, is not the correct view. The Doctrine and Discipline (*dharma* and *vināya*), Ananda, which I have taught and enjoined upon you is to be your Teacher when I am gone. But whereas now, Ananda, all the *bhikkhus* address each other with the title of "friend" (*avuso*), not so must they address each other after I am gone. A senior *bhikkhu*, Ananda, is to address a junior *bhikkhu* by his given name, or by his family name, or by the title of "friend"; a junior *bhikkhu* is to address a senior *bhikkhu* with the title "reverend Sir" (*Bhānte*) or "venerable."[20]

In an important *sutra* included in the *Majjhima Nikāya* (*Sutra* 26) the Buddha gives an account of his life and a succinct summary of the essentials of his teachings. In a description of the events after his enlightenment the Buddha narrates his encounter with the band of five monks, who had parted company with him when he gave up extreme authorities for he found them to be pointless mortifications of the body. These five ascetics had left him as they took the future Buddha's moderate attitude as his return to a life of luxury. When the Buddha met these ascetics at the deer-park (Sarnath) at the outskirts of Varanasi, they gave him a reluctant welcome and addressed him by name and by the title "friend." This is how the Buddha admonished them before blessing them with his very first sermon:

> O, *Bhikkhus*, address not the Tathāgata by his name, nor by the title of "Friend." An *Arhat*, O, *Bhikkhus* is the Tathāgata, a supreme Buddha. Give ear, O *Bhikkhus*. The deathless has been gained, and I will instruct you and teach you the *Dharma* . . . that highest good to which the holy life conducts, and for the sake of which youths of good family so nobly retire from the household life to the houseless one.[21]

The Buddha did not reprove the ascetics out of haughtiness or due to a lack of humility, but out of a realization that without *bhakti* and *bhakti's* attendant code of conduct, a philosophy will fall short of *dharma*. He knew that the flower of *jñāna* looses its fragrance without *bhakti*. Bhakti makes philosophy a living philosophy.

BHAKTI IN THE *MĀHAPARINIBBĀNA SUTTA*

Mahāparinibbāna Sutta is one of the largest *sutras* in the *Dīgha Nikāya* sections of the Pali canon. This is the largest of the larger *sutras* included in the *Dīgha Nikāya* and gives an account of the events leading up to the Buddha's demise. Initially transmitted by way of an oral tradition, the Pali canon is supposed to have been committed to writing around first century B.C. in Sri Lanka. *Mahāparinibbāna Sutta*, besides tracing the events of the last three months of the Buddha's life, offers a recapitulation of the essentials of the Buddha's message, a succinct summary of his mission and a snapshot of the social and political conditions of the times (circa 500 B.C.) in which the historical Buddha carried out his ministry. Obviously it also offers a snapshot of the bhakti ethos of the times as well as of the bhakti that was an integral component of the *dharma*, *sangha* (the Buddhist church, community of monks), and *vināya* (discipline) as defined, approved, and set into motion by the Buddha himself. In some of its features the *Mahāparinibbāna Sutta* is very much compatable to Plato's *Phaedo* in which the last moments of Socrates's life and a recapitulation of his philosophical mission are reported.

The personal bond of bhakti and the *guru-şişya* (teacher-disciple) relationship between the Buddha and Ananda is comparable to the similar intimacy between Kŗşņa and Arjuna in the *Bhagavadgita*. Just as in the *Gita* and in the *Phaedo*, the human drama is intertwined with the philosophical message very impressively in *Mahāparinibbāna Sutta*. The poetry, the pathos, the appeal to human heart that these texts combine with their respective philosophical and religious systems has placed them among the true classics of world literature. Their ability to transmit a deeper and truly existential message between the lines could not have been accomplished by their authors without the invocation of bhakti, the handmaiden of all *jñāna* (fundamental knowledge), already present as a familiar practice in their worlds.

The text of the *Mahāparinibbāna Sutta* is divided into six chapters or "portions for recitation." In the first chapter the Buddha is shown as staying in Rajagraha (Rajgiri) on a hill called the Vulture's Peak. The text opens with a description of how Ajatashatru, the King of Magadha sent a Brahmin emissary, his prime minister, to consult with the Buddha concerning the king's impending hostilities with the confederacy of the Vajjians. Ajatashatru, just as his father Bimbisara before him, was the chief patron of the Buddha. Another well-wisher of the Buddha was King Prasenajit of Kausala in whose territory, especially in his capital city Sravasti (Svatthi) he had delivered numerous discourses. Kausala had also suzerainty over the Sakya Republic of which Gautama was a prince. Throughout the *sutra*, the Buddha is shown as moving from one place to the other, as if staying in one place for too long was not desirable for him as a *śrmana* (*samana*, wandering monk). Modern historians of ancient India point out that in the times of the Buddha, the agrarian and pastoral society had given way to well-functioning states including republics called the *gaṇa-sanghas* with numerous *rājas* electing their governing councils and powerful monarchies such as Magatha and Kausala. Buddhist texts show a chronological accuracy as well as accurate historical data with respect to the states, cities, and events although just like the Hindu texts and religious histories (*purāna*) provide no accurate dates. According to John Keay, a time-lapse between the India of later Vedic texts such as the *Upanishads* and the earliest Buddhist and Jain texts is obvious.

> The Sanskrit texts evoke a mostly agrarian way of life in which states play a minor part and status is governed by lineage and ritual observance. Buddhist and Jain texts, on the other hand, portray a network of functioning states, each with an urban nucleus heavily engaged in trade and production. It allows room for the evolution of a tradition of heterodoxy and dissent. Buddhist texts in particular portray a society that was already in religious ferment when the Buddha was born. Rival holy-men swarm across the countryside performing feats of endurance, disputing one another's spiritual credentials and vying with one another for followers and patronage . . . (Kautilya's) *Arthasastra* recognizes such renunciates as an important constituent of any state; they are to be given legal protection and free passage; special forest areas are to be allotted to them for meditation, and special lodging-houses in the city. . . . The philosophies on offer from this ragtag army of reformers ranged from mind-boggling mysticism to defiant nihilism and blank agnosticism, from the outright materialism of the Lokayats (*Cārvākas*) to the heavy determinism of the Ajivikas, from the rationalism of the Buddha to the esoterism of Mahavira. Most, however, agreed in condemning the extravagance of the Vedic sacrifice, in sidelining the Vedic pantheon, and in ignoring Brahmanical authority.[22]

What Keay describes about the fifth-century B.C. India with respect to the rise of monarchical states, of mercantile classes and trade, the breakdown of the caste-system and the authority of the priestly caste, the culmination of the heterodox tendencies and fringe groups into well-organized philosophical systems and religious order is visible in the *sutras* of early Buddhism. That a culture of *guru-bhakti* was in place due to the existence of so many spiritual masters of different persuasions, each having followers of his own but at the same time practicing an open-door policy toward the followers of others can be gleaned from these *sutras*. That the monks and lay followers of different sects interacted peacefully with each other, held religious and philosophical debates with each other, and practiced a general decorum of bhakti toward the masters of all sects, is also revealed in a perusal of these texts. For instance, the *Mahāparinibbāna Sutta* describes that the wandering monk Subhadda who shows up to discuss a religious matter on the very last day of the Buddha on this earth refers to the Buddha as "Samana Gautama" instead of the Blessed One (*Bhagavān*), but exchanges the same "compliments of esteem and civility" with the master as the other *bhikkhus* habitually did. "He was the last disciple whom the Blessed One himself converted" according to the *sutra*.

The *Mahāparinibbāna Sutta* (MPS) begins with the emissary of the King Ajatashatru approaching the Buddha seeking his reactions to the prospect of an impending war with the Vajjian confederacy. The King sends his prime minister to the Buddha with the following instructions: "Come now, O Brahmin, do you go to the Blessed One and bow down in adoration at his feet on my behalf, and enquire in my name whether he is . . . in vigorous health. . . . And bear carefully in mind whatever the Blessed One may predict, and repeat it to me. For the Buddhas speak nothing untrue."[23] When the Buddha is apprised of Ajatashatru's plans to attack the Vajjians by Brahmin Vassakara, the Buddha remarks to Ananda, who "was standing behind the Blessed One, and fanning him" that as long as the Vajjians hold

> full and frequent public assemblies, . . . meet together in accord . . . so long as they enact nothing not already established . . . act according to the ancient institutions . . . so long as they revere and support the Vajjian elders . . . so long as no women and girls . . . are detained by force or abduction . . . so long as they honour Vajjian shrines . . . so long as the rightful protection, defence and support shall be fully provided for the *arhats* among them, so that *arhats* from a distance may enter the realm and the *arhats* therein may live at ease—so long may the Vajjians be expected not to decline but to prosper. (*MPS*, p. 4)

It is noteworthy that the Buddha can speak his mind fearlessly about a matter that affects the king personally. The Buddha is staying in the outskirts of the city, Rajagraha, the capital of this king. Speaking through his personal assistant, the Venerable Ananda, who has served him with unsurpassable bhakti for over twenty-five years and who is "standing behind the Blessed One, fanning him," as the Brahmin prime minister approaches him. The Buddha remarks that so long as the Vajjians follow some democratic norms ("full and frequent public assemblies"), expected of the *gaṇa-sanghas* having ruling-councils rather than one-man rule, and lived in concord—discord was too easy for the Vajjian confederacy, for theirs was a union of eight different clans—they were expected to prosper. The Buddha also stipulated that so long as the Vajjians acted according to their institutional orders, revered their elders, did not use force against girls and women, and honored their shrines, they were likely to do well and hold their own against external aggression. The Buddha did not fail to mention that welcoming, hosting, and protecting the *arhats*, giving them safe passage from one state to the other was a paramount requirement of a civilized society. He was echoing one of the important attributes of a state mentioned in Kautilya's *Arthāsastra* (third century B.C.) and described as follows by the historian John Keay, quoted above: "*Arthasastra* recognizes such renunciates as an important constituent of any state; they are to be given legal protection and free passage." Religious masters, *şrmanas*, *brahmins*, and *arhats* were given reverence across the sectarian boundaries and across state borders. The culture of bhakti was not confined to the orthodox Vedic Brahmanism sections of Hinduism, but several heterodox sects led by masters often hailing from non-Brahmin castes—the Buddha and Mahavira were both *kştriyas*, and many śŗmana chiefs were non-Brahmins—all having scanty regard for Vedic rituals and the caste system as such, were all glorious practitioners of bhakti. They had plenty of *guru-bhakti*, humanism, compassion, and consideration for the common man's weal and woe and salvation, and offered an unritualistic and unmediated versions of religion. These are all time-honored features of the practice of bhakti.

After the visit of the Magadhan prime minister, the Buddha delivers a discourse to the assembled *bhikkhus* of the Rajgraha area, and delivered a discourse on the "seven conditions of the welfare of a community," a code of conduct for the *bhikkhus* of the Buddhist *sangha* (order). Three conditions are the modified version of the same conditions mentioned to Brahmin Vassakara with respect to the Vajjians. In addition another set of "seven conditions of welfare" are mentioned also to be practiced by the *bhikkhus*. These are: refraining from business (*bhikkhus* are not supposed to be businessmen or merchants), idle talk, slothfulness, social merrymaking, sinful desires, company of sinful persons, and any stopping on their way to *nirvana*. It is noteworthy that in his sermons to the Magadha prime minister as well as to the group (*sangha*) of *bhikkhus* the Buddha lays emphasis on conduct or the ways of life, and not just a theoretical elucidation of *dharma*. In a way he was expounding on a bhakti way of life, so essential to any noble religion or civilized society.

The Buddha's movements from one place to the other, even at the age of eighty, were so spontaneous and compassionate, consistent with the life of a *şrmana* and of one devoted so personally to his mission. He wrote nothing, but he wrote so indelibly on the hearts and minds of the people blessed with his company.

> Now when the Blessed One had sojourned at Rajagaha as long as he pleased, he addressed the Venerable Ananda, and said: Come, Ananda, let us go to Ambalathika.
>
> So be it Lord! Said Ananda in assent, and the Blessed One, with a large company of the *bhikkhus*, proceeded to Ambalatthika. (*MPS*, p. 12)

From Ambalatthika, the Buddha moves to Nalanda, where he has a "comprehensive religious talk with the *bhikkhus* on the nature of upright conduct, *samādhi* (contemplation) and intelligence." From thereon he continues his (last) journey to Pataligama (later to be Patliputra). At Pataligama he delivers a discourse on the "five-fold loss of the wrong-doer" to a group of householders, local disciples and the *bhikkhus*. The assembly is dismissed as follows:

> The night is far spent, O householders. It is time for you to do what you deem most fit. "Even so Lord!" answered the disciples of Patligama, and they rose from their seats, and bowing to the Blessed One, and keeping him on their right hand as they passed him, they departed thence. (*MPS*, p. 17)

That a code of conduct of devotion to ascetics and spiritual stalwarts of all persuasions was in place in those times, is quite visible to a reader of this *sutra*. The visit by the Arhat Buddha on his last journey was no ordinary event. At Pataligama, the Buddha along with his retinue of *bhikkhus* is invited to the home of Brahmans Vassakara and Sunidha, the chief ministers of Magadha, who were overseeing the construction of a fortress, "to keep back the Vajjins." After the meal, the "ministers brought a low seat and sat down respectfully at his (the Buddha's) side." Seated on a higher seat the Buddha "gave thanks in these verses":

> Wheresoever the prudent man shall take up his abode
> Let him support there good and upright men of self-control.
> Let him give gifts to all deities as may be there
> Revered, they will revere him: honoured they will honour him again;
> Are gracious to him as a mother to her own, her only son.
> And a man who has the grace of gods, good fortune he beholds. (*MPS*, p. 20)

T. W. Rhys Davids, the translator of the *MPS* mentions in a footnote that this passage gives the commentator Buddhaghosa (fifth century A.D.) "a good deal of difficulty" for offerings to the gods, is clearly inconsistent with the Buddha's (new) *dharma*. Rhys Davids resolves the difficulty by suggesting, on the grounds of the *Deva-dhamma Jataka* story number 9, that by "deities" is meant "the good and upright men of self-control." I am inclined to believe however, that the Buddha was repeating a popular verse, exhorting people to continue to show bhakti toward *arhats*, *brahmins*, and ascetics, these "good and upright men of self-control," and have their new dwelling quarters blessed by a visit of such a holy man, soon after its construction. The Buddha was not referring to a code of conduct for the "Buddhist" *bhikkhus* and householders alone, but people of all persuasions living in a culture of bhakti. Obviously his host Vassakara, the Brahmin, was not a member of the Buddhist order, but a Brahmin by caste, appointed as the prime minister by King Ajatashatru. Regarding why the Buddha refers to the "upright men of self-control" (*arhats*) and gods in the same breath, the following passage from *Śvetāśvatara-Upanishad* quoted by us in chapter 1, is instructive. This passage offers the first usage of the term *bhakti* in Vedic literature, although the verb *bhaj* and several synonyms of bhakti were widely used in the *Vedas* and *Upanishads*.

> To one who has the bhakti for a god (*deva*)
> And for a teacher (*guru*) even as for god (*deva*)
> To him these matters become manifest.[24]

Thus the Buddha compliments and thanks his hosts by remarking that having one's new place of residence blessed by an *arhat* is tantamount to paying homage to the gods. These "upright men of self-control" (*arhat*, guru, saint) as well the gods, when revered, will revere back their devotee, and when honored will honor back, when loved will love you back like a mother loves her only son. This is a statement concerning the method of bhakti. It is a two-way love. A person loves the deity, like he loves a beloved person. The deity will love its devotee back. This two-way love is shown existing between Kṛṣṇa, the divine Being, and Arjuna, the man in the *Bhagavadgita*. The Buddha is expressing the bhakti faith: when one loves, one will be loved back. This applies to the devotee's relationship to the *arhats* and to the gods (*devas*) alike.

In chapter 2 of the *MPS*, the Buddha moves on to the village called Kotigama and affirms in a discourse to the *bhikkhus* that wandering through transmigrations of rebirth take place for those who have not understood and grasped the four noble truths. Soon afterward the Buddha and his retinue move on the village of Nadika, and after a conversation with Ananda on the fates of some recently deceased *bhikkhus* of the area and usual discourses on "the nature of upright conduct," the Buddha leads his company of *bhikkhus* to the great city of Vaisali (*MPS*, p. 28) the capital of the Licchavi republic of Vajjian confederacy of which the Licchavians were the principal clan. Licchavians had a history of hostilities with Magadha. It is interesting to notice the ease with which the Buddha's group moves to Licchavi republic, an enemy territory for the state of Magadha. At Vaisali, the Buddha stays at Ambapali's grove, as a guest of the courtesan Ambapali, the Indian Helen of Troy, who had secretly hosted the enemy, king Bimbisara, the father of Ajatashatru, and had added fuel to the fire of a protracted war between Licchavis and the Magadhans. Ambapali was an influential, rich, and shrewd lady but she was after all a courtesan. According to *MPS*, soon after the Buddha's arrival in Vaisali she comes to see him and invites him and the *bhikkhus* to her house for a meal. "And the Blessed One gave, by silence, his consent" (*MPS*, p. 30). Now several Licchavi princes and royal families also arrive with a great pomp and show with the intention of inviting the Buddha to their palace. On their way they run into Ambapali's caravan and try to bribe her to "give up this meal for a hundred thousand." But she would not give up "so honourable a feast" even if she was offered the entire Vaisali with its subject territories. Licchavi's exclaim "we are outdone by this mango-girl! We are out-reached by this mango-girl!" for the word "ambapali" literally means "the grower of mangoes." When the Licchavis pay their obeisance to the Buddha, they are also blessed with a discourse, but he does not accept their invitation for a meal, which was already promised to Ambapali. The Buddha's overlooking of the dishonorable profession of this woman and treating her the same way as he would a prince (*raja*) is comparable to Christ's compassionate treatment of Mary Magdalene.

From Ambapali's grove, the Buddha travels on to the village of Beluva and while there he asks the *bhikkhus* to go on to stay with their relatives and friends around Vaisali for the duration of the rainy season. It was here in Beluva that "there fell upon him a dire sickness and sharp pains came upon him" (*MPS,* p. 35). But since he did not want to pass away without addressing the *bhikkhus* and without "taking leave of the *sangha*," he bent down the sickness with a strong will. When Ananda voices his expectation that the Blessed One ought to leave instructions concerning the order (*sangha*), the Buddha responds:

> What then Ananda, the Order expect of me? I have preached the truth (*dharma*) without making any distinction between exoteric or esoteric doctrine: for in respect of the truths, Ananda, the Tathāgata has no such thing as the closed fist of a teacher, who keeps things back.
>
> Therefore Ananda, be ye lamps unto yourselves. Be ye refuge to yourselves. Betake yourselves to no external refuge. Hold fast to the *dharma* as a lamp. Hold fast as a refuge to *dharma*. Look not for refuge to anyone besides yourselves. (*MPS*, p. 38)

Here the Buddha reminds Ananda, that the cardinal principle of Buddhism is self-discovery to the point of a realization of no-self. To dismiss all external authority, even that of the Buddha is required for a practitioner of Buddhism. The four noble truths, the essence of the Buddha's *dharma*, are "the constitution of things" and not the by-product of the Buddha. The Buddha is not the author of the truth, he is merely the teacher who indicates and elucidates the truth. As the sutra (III–1341) from the *Anguttara Nikāya*, quoted earlier in this chapter, says:

> Whether the Buddhas arise, O Bhikkhus, or whether the Buddhas do not arise, it remains a fact and the fixed and necessary constitution of being that all its constituents are transitory . . . that all its constituents are *dukkhā* (pain) . . . that all its elements are *anattā* (soul-less).

> This fact a Buddha discovers and masters, and when he has discovered and mastered it, he announces, teaches, publishes, proclaims, discloses, minutely explains, makes it clear, that all the constituents of being are . . . transitory . . . *dukkhā* . . . and *anattā*.[25]

In other words, while the Buddha reminds Ananda that he has nothing more spectacular to say to the Order (*sangha*) over and above what he has already been "teaching, minutely explaining and making clear" for over forty-five years, he is exhorting his disciples to rise above the "*saguṇa* bhakti" (devotion of a Being with attributes, i.e., a personal lord) to a "*nirguṇa* bhakti" (devotion of an attributeless Being) of the *dharma* itself. While he did not recommend getting rid of personal devotion toward the elders, saints, *arhats,* and *ṣrmanas*, which was and continues to be embedded in the culture of India, he asked his *bhikkhus* to be self-reliant and "lamps unto themselves" and let *dharma* be their guide, refuge, and teacher, after their embodied teacher is gone. He asked them to rise above mere "saguṇa bhakti" to a mature "nirguṇa bhakti" for human beings are more in need of internal lawfulness than external teachings. This also reflects the emphasis on the "individual quest" that has endeared Buddhism forever to thoughtful minds beyond sectarian and national boundaries.

In chapter 3 of the *MPS*, the Buddha is shown as spending a day in Kalpa Ketia, a place in the vicinity of Vaisali. This is where some supernatural events take place, as the Buddha "deliberately and consciously rejects the rest of his allotted sum of life" (*MPS*, p. 44). A mighty earthquake came soon after the Buddha communicates his decision to Buddhist devil, Mara, who had been paying frequent visits during the times, the Buddha was left alone by Ananda. Mara had been urging the Buddha to pass away as soon as possible. The Buddha finally obliges him:

> O Evil One! Make yourself happy, the Final extinction of the Tathāgata shall take place before long. At the end of three months from this time the Tathāgata will die. (*MPS*, p. 44)

The invoking of the supernatural, the visits of Mara, the homage and the lamentation of innumerable gods when they learn of the Tathāgata's death and descend on earth to witness the great decease, are of course the embellishments added by the composers and subsequent writers of the *sutra*. All this is, of course, indicative of the bhakti of the *bhikkhus* and disciples of the Buddha toward him. Such elements should not affect either the philosophical merit or the historical value of this document. The mythos goes hand in hand with logos in all ancient philosophical as well as scriptural texts of all traditions.

Buddhist texts are no exception. In the midst of such supernatural allusions Ananda is given this remarkable philosophical thought:

> But now Ananda, have I not formerly declared to you that it is the very nature of all things, near and dear unto us, that we must divide ourselves from them? How then, Ananda, can this be possible—whereas anything whatever born, brought into being, and organized, contains within itself the inherent necessity of dissolution—how then can this be possible that such a being should not be dissolved? (*MPS*, p. 59)

The Buddha is pointing out that bhakti devoid of knowledge (*jñāna, dharma*) can easily become "attachment" leading to the pain of separation. Knowledge of *dharma* (the law) reminds us that we must "divide ourselves" from those "near and dear unto us." *Dharma* (Truth) tells us that all component things must dissolve, and thus separation is inevitable for all meetings and all relationships. Thus, the Buddha tells the *bhikkhus* in the Kutagara Hall in Mahavana: "Behold now, *Bhikkhus*, I exhort you. All component things must decay. Work out your nibbana with diligence" (*MPS*, p. 61). All things, including living things are doomed to perish. That is, however, no reason to sit still and be disheartened. The struggle for salvation, the ultimate good, the ultimate freedom, must be undertaken, and must continue despite the transitoriness all around.

MPS, chapter 4, begins with the Buddha's last sojourn in Vaisali and from there he moves to Bhanda-gama, where he delivers a discourse to the *bhikkhus*. From then on he passes through the villages of Amba-gama and Gambu-gama, and arrives in Bhoga-nagara, where he addresses the *bhikkhus* on the issue of how his teachings that are presented after his passing are to be compared with scriptures for their authenticity. This indicates that some written scriptures were available in the Buddha's lifetime. As T. W. Rhy Davids explains in his book *Buddhist India*, such "comparing with scriptures" may have meant consulting with those *bhikkhus* who had perfectly memorized the entire *sutra*. Since

> The idea of recording, by writing even a *suttanta* . . . did not occur to the men who composed or used the canonical texts. . . . The Indian people had been acquainted with letters, and with writing, for a long time, probably for centuries before; and had made very general use of writing for short communications. It seems extraordinary that they should have abstained from its use on occasions, which were to them so important (such as preserving the scriptures).[26]

Although a century or two after the demise of the Buddha the Buddhist councils will decide to commit the *sutras* of various lengths to writing. Initially they were composed in a style, replete with repetitious passages that are easy for commission to memory and recitation. This is why the chapters of the *MPS* are called "recitations." It was part and parcel of the bhakti ethos that the most sublime literature be memorized by heart and passed on by word of mouth. Writing and reading were considered less than perfect mediums for religious discourse. What one loves, adores, and reveres ought to be in one's heart, effortlessly memorized, not buried dead in a book. This is why the Buddha, like Socrates and Christ, chose to write on the hearts of the people. Personal contact which is an important ingredient of bhakti was so important to him that he was traveling relentlessly even in the last few months of his life to reach out to people. This was his bhakti toward his people, who will later record and spread his word by the sheer dynamism of bhakti.

After spending some time in Bhoga-nagara, the Buddha, "with a great company of the *bhikkhus*" proceeded to Pava. In Pava he stayed at the mango grove of Chunda, the metalworker. At a meal in Chunda's house the Buddha partakes a certain dish called *sukara-maddava,* which caused dire sickness, dysentery and sharp pains. But the Buddha bore the pain without complaint, and soon afterwards advised Ananda and the group of *bhikkhus* to accompany him to Kusinara. Since the word *sukra* means "pig," Rhys Davids translates *sukara-maddava* as "dried boar's flesh." It could also mean, a dish of "soft boiled rice with five dairy products" or a kind of alchemistic elixir or "young bamboo shoots trampled by pigs (*sukarehi maddita-vamsakaliro*, vide Dharmapala's commentary)." According to *Rajanigantu*, an Indian compendium of medicinal plants, there are many plants beginning with the term *sukara*.[27] Thus it is by no means certain that the Buddha was a nonvegetarian. In any case the Buddha had a dire sickness after eating Chunda's meal. And yet he was not willing to give up his lifestyle of a *śrmana*; his missionary activity was resumed the next day.

Chapter 5 of the *MPS* describes that the Buddha proceeded to the Sala grove of the Mallas. He asks Ananda to spread a couch between the sala trees so that he can lie down. After eating Chunda's meal during his travels, he had frequently requested that a robe be folded in order for him to rest a while. The *sutra* describes that the sala trees blossoms forth out of season and innumerable heavenly hosts, gods, and spirits of the ten world systems came to behold the Tathāgata. While spirits "of the worldly mind" lamented the prospect of Buddha's passing, other spirits that were "free from passion" bore it calmly saying "Impermanent indeed are all component things . . ." (*MPS*, p. 90). After this visitation by the deities (*devata*) of the sky, Ananda says regretfully to the Buddha that after his demise, the *bhikkhus* from far and wide, who used to come to visit the Buddha after the end of the rainy season, will have no one to pay obeisance to. The Buddha responds that the believers should visit four places associated with him, namely, where the Tathāgata was born, where he attained enlightenment, where he set the wheel of *dharma* moving (*dharma cakka ppavattana*), and where he attained his *pari nibbāna*.

> And there will come, Ananda, to such spots believers, *bhikkhus* and *bhikkhnnis* of the order, devout men and devout women (*upasaka* and *upasakayio*), and will say here was the Tathāgata born, . . . here the Tathāgata passed away. . . . (*MPS*, p. 91)

Here the Buddha is shown as making sure that after his passing, the bhakti practices on the part of the *bhikkhus* and devotees of either sex, continue unabated. Instead of seeking audience (*darṣana*) of the Buddha after the conclusion of the rainy season, the *bhikkhus* and lay devotees alike shall make pilgrimage to places where the major events of Buddha's career took place. The term used for the devotees from the general public who are not ordained as *bhikkhus* is *upāsaka*, *upāsana* (devotion, worship) being a synonym of *bhakti*. Thus the Buddha did not want the flame of bhakti to extinguish after his passing. For bhakti is so essential to the practice of *dharma*.

> What are we to do Lord (*Bhānte*) with the remains (*sarira*; body) of the Tathāgata? Hinder not yourself Ananda, by honouring the remains (*sirira pūja*) of the Tathāgata. Be zealous, I beseech you Ananda, in your own behalf. . . . There are wise-men (*pandita*) among Brahmins, among the nobles (*ksatriyas*) among heads of households (*gahapati*), who are firm believers (*abhippasanna*) in the Tathāgata; and they will do honour to the remains (*sarirapujam*) of the Tathāgata. (*MPS*, p. 91)

This conversation between the Buddha and Ananda is comparable to the one between Socrates and Crito (*Phaedo*, 115b). When Crito asked on behalf of all friends of Socrates what they were to do after Socrates's death, he responded "Nothing new. . . . Just what I have always been telling you. Just look to yourselves." The terms *abhipassanna* and *puja* (from *sarirapuja*) are again synonyms of *bhakti*. Buddha is sure that authoritative persons whether *brahmins* or *ksatriyas* or heads of households will worship (*pūja*) his relics appropriately. Ananda however should look to his own journey toward *nirvana*.

The personal bond of love and bhakti between the Buddha and Ananda, appears poignantly in chapter 5 of the *MPS*, when the Buddha inquires about Ananda's whereabouts.

> The venerable Ananda, Lord, has gone into the *Vihāra* (pavilion), and stands leaning against the lintel of the door, and weeping at the thought: Alas, I remain still but a learner, one who has still to work out his perfection. And the Master is about to pass away from me—he who is so kind to me (*mam anukampako*). (*MPS*, p. 96)

The Buddha gently admonishes his constant companion of the past twenty-five years, who weeps just as excitable Appolodoros does for Socrates in *The Phaede*:

> Enough Ananda. Do not let yourself be troubled; do not weep. Have I not, on former occasions told you that it is in the very nature of all things most near and dear unto us that we must divide ourselves from them, leave them, sever ourselves from them. . . . (*MPS*, p. 96)

When people in the neighborhood, the Mallas of Kusinara are informed of the impending death of the Buddha in their own village, their reaction shows their deep love for him:

> The Mallas with their young men and maidens and their wives were grieved, and sad, and afflicted at heart. And some of them wept, disheveling their hair, and stretched forth their arms and wept, fell prostrate on the ground, and rolled to and fro in anguish at the thought: "Too soon will the Blessed One die. Too soon will the happy one pass away. Full soon will the Eye of the world (*chakkhu-loke*) vanish away." (*MPS*, p. 102)

In the evening the Mallas get their audience (*darşana*) with the Buddha, as Ananda presents them one family at a time so that the maximum number of people receive the blessing of witnessing (*darşana*) the Tathāgata in person. Soon afterward a local ascetic Subaddha shows up to see the Buddha seeking resolution of a religious issue. Considering the Buddha's state of health and his hectic schedule with the Mallas, he is denied an audience by Ananda. However, Subaddha persists in his request for a meeting. The Buddha overhears this and asks Ananda to let Subaddha talk to him. This willingness to discuss philosophy shortly before the hour of death, reminds us of the similar decision taken by Socrates when he chose to discuss philosophy with his friends on his death-day. Subaddha who addresses the Buddha as "*Samana Gautama*" rather than "*Bhagavān*" wants to know whether the doctrines of the rival "*Śrmana-brahmins*" (*Śrmanas* deserving the title of *brahmins*), such as Purāna Kassapa, Makkhali, Ajita, Kaccayana, Sanjya, and Nigantha, have understood the Truth. The Buddha asks him to let the matter of the truth-value of the rival sectarian doctrines rest. But he should know that the Buddha's *dharma* is the only one that offers the noble eightfold path and is the only one in which true saints (*arhats*) are to be found. This *dharma* has been founded so that "the *bhikkhus* may live a life that is right (*samma*), so that the world may not be bereft of *arhats*" (p. 107). Subaddha decides to join the Order. "He was the last disciple whom the Blessed One himself converted" (*MPS,* p. 110).

The sixth and the last chapter of *MPS* begin with the Buddha's instructions to Ananda concerning the state of the Order (*sangha*) after the Buddha's demise. Some *bhikkhus* might think that "the word of the teacher is ended, we have no teacher anymore." But that is not the right attitude. The Buddha wishes the doctrine and the discipline (*dharma* and *vināya*) be the teacher, after his passing (*MPS,* p. 112). The Master made sure that decorum of bhakti is maintained within the *sangha*:

> Ananda, when I am gone address not one another in the way in which the *bhikkhus* have heretofore addressed each other—with the epithet, that is, of *avuso* (Friend). A younger *bhikkhu* may be addressed by an elder (*thera*) with his name or family name, or the title "Friend." But an elder should be addressed by a younger *bhikkhu* as "Lord" (*Bhante*) or as "Venerable Sir" (*Ayasma*). (*MPS*, p. 112)

Then the Buddha inquires from the assembly of *bhikkhus* whether any one of them has any doubt or misgiving concerning the Buddha, or the Dharma, or the *sangha* or the *magga* (the path). He is very pleased to know that not a single *bikkhu* had any misgivings.

> Then the Blessed One addressed the *bhikkhus*, and said, Behold now, *bhikkhus*, I exhort you, saying, "Decay is inherent in all component things. Work out your salvation with diligence." This was the last word of the Tathāgata. (*MPS,* p. 114)

A more literal translation of the Buddha's last word should be:

> All component things have the nature of decay; strive earnestly (*vayadhamma sankhara; appamadena sampadetha*).

These last words of the Buddha offer Buddhism in a nutshell. "Decay is inherent in all component things" expresses the fundamental insight of Buddhism that "all is transitory." But this is no reason to relax one's striving for perfection, which must continue without any lapse of alertness. With full mindfulness, we must strive toward the goal, that is, *nirvana*. Buddhaghosa explains in his commentary that this exhortation means "you should accomplish all your duties without allowing mindfulness to lapse" for *appamada* means "presence of mindfulness."

The people of the area, Mallas of Kusinara were informed of the Buddha's demise. They reacted with much lamentation and subsequently took charge of the funeral arrangements. His body was cremated with full honors as the "remains of a king of kings" ought to be treated. The body was committed to flames after a week upon the arrival of Maha Kassappa with a great company of *bhikkhus*. For another seven days the Mallas paid homage to the ashes. As the news of the Buddha's demise spread, messengers came from the King Ajatashatru of Magatha, the Licchavis of Vaisali, the Sakyas of Kapil-vastu, the Bullis of Allakappa, Koliyas of Ramagama, Brahmin of Vethadipa, and the Mallas of Pava. All of them laid claims to the relics of the Buddha. Dona, the Brahmin urged the various claimants to calm down with the words:

Unseemly is it that over the division
Of the remains of him who was the best of beings
Strife should arise, and wounds and war.
Let us sirs, with one accord unite
In friendly harmony to make eight portions
Widespread let *stūpas* arise in every land
That in the Enlightened One mankind may trust. (*MPS,* p.133)

The Moriyas, the Magadhans, the Licchavis, the Bullis, the Koliyas, Vethadipaka the Brahmin, the Mallas of Pava, and the Mallas of Kusinara, all erected *stūpas* (memorial mounds) over the relics, and Dona the Brahman made a *stūpa* over the vessel that contained the ashes. The Buddha had correctly predicted to Ananda that kings and chieftains from Brahmin and Kṣtriyas castes will pay due homage to his remains.

ENDNOTES

1. Nicol Macnicol, *Indian Theism.* (New Delhi: Munshilal Manoharlal, 1915).
2. B. G. Gokhale, "Bhakti in Early Buddhism," in J. Lele, ed., *Tradition and Modernity in Bhakti Movements.* (Leiden, Netherlands: E. J. Brill, 1991).
3. *Anguttara-nikaya*, pp. iii, 134, in H. C. Warren, trans. *Buddhism in Translations*, (Cambridge, Mass.: Harvard University Press, 1953), p. xiv. Hereafter abbreviated *BT.*
4. M. Dhavamony, *Love of God According to Saiva Siddhanta.* (London: Oxford University Press, 1971), pp. 11–45. Dhavamony offers a comprehensive etymological analysis of the term "bhakti."
5. *Ibid.*, p. 20.
6. *Rig Veda*, 1.156.3; 8.32.14; 9.113.14; 9.113.2; 10.151.2, 3.7.
7. *Rig Veda*, 8.32.14; 9.113.2, 4; 10.151.2, 3.7.
8. R. G. Bhandarkav, *Vaishavism, Saivism and Minor Religions Systems.* (Strausberg, Germany: K. J. Trubner, 1913) pp. 54–58.
9. S. R. Goyal, *A Religious History of India.* Vol. I (Meerut, India: Kusumanjali, 1984), pp. 133–62.
10. *Majjhima-nikaya,* 63, in *BT*, pp. 117–22.
11. Vinoba Bhave, *Talks on the Gita.* (New York: Macmillan, 1960).
12. *Mulamadhyamaka-kārika*, XV.7, in David J. Kalupahana. Trans. *Nagarjuna: The Philosophy of the Middle Way* (Albany, N.Y.: State University of New York Press, 1986), p. 232.
13. "The Introduction to the Jataka," 1–47–21; *BT*, p. 40.
14. *Samyutta-Nikāya*, 13–35–1; *BT*, p. 162.

15. Ibid.

16. "Prabodha-Candrodaya" by Krsna Misra, trans. J. Taylor; S. Radhakrishnan, and C. A. Moore, ed. *A Sourcebook in Indian Philosophy* (Princeton, N.J.: Princeton University Press, 1957), p. 247.

17. Ibid., p. 248.

18. *Sumangala-Vilasini*, 1–45–10; *BT*, p. 92.

19. *Dhamma-cakka-ppavattana Sutta*; T. W. Rhys Davids, trans. *Buddhist Suttas* (New York: Dover, 1969), p. 148.

20. *Māha-parinibbāna Sutta*; *BT*, p. 107.

21. *Majjhima-Nikaya*, Sutta 26; *BT*, p. 344.

22. John Keay, *India: A History* (London: Folio Society, 2003), Vol. I, pp. 71, 72.

23. "Mahaparinibbana Sutta," in T. W. Rhys Davids, trans. *Buddhist Suttas* (New York: Dover, 1969), p. 2. Hereafter abbreviated *MPS.*

24. *Śvetāsvatara Upanishad*, 6–23.

25. *BT,* p. XIV.

26. T. W. Rhys Davids, *Buddhist India* (New Delhi: Munshiram Manoharlal, 1999), p. 112.

27. Sister Vajira and Francis Story, trans. *Last Days of the Buddha: The Māha-parinibbāna Sutta* (Kandy, Sri Lanka: Buddhist Publication Society, 1998), p. 95.

3

Bhakti and Philosophy in the *Bhagavadgita*

Bhagavadgita is one of the best known and the most authoritative texts of the Hindu tradition and has come to be regarded as one of the jewels of the world's philosophical, religious, and literary masterpieces. Its conciseness, structural neatness, conceptual harmony, as well as its lucid summation of the preceding and contemporary schools of thought, along with the originality of its own system, are its outstanding merits. Together with the *Upanishads* and the *Brahma Sutras*, it is regarded as one of the triple cannon (*prasthāna-traya*) and given the distinction of being "the last Upanishad." Thus not only the exponents of the various branches of the *Vedānta* school, but those of the other schools of Hindu thought have written classical commentaries on the *Gita*. The exact date and authorship of the text is unknown, as is the case with many other works of the Vedic tradition. It is estimated that the work was composed sometime between the fifth and the second century B.C.[1] It is certainly a post-Upanishadic and post-Buddhistic text since it summarizes the insights of and quotes from the classical *Upanishads* and refers to early Buddhism. The author of the *Gita* is obviously familiar enough with the classical systems of *Sāṁkhya* and *Yoga* since he harmonizes the viewpoints of both into a unified doctrine. He also names and briefly describes several other contemporary religio-philosophical traditions.

The authorship is generally attributed to Vyasa, the compiler of the epic *Māhabhārata*, of which *Gita* constitutes a section. The eighteen chapters of the *Gita* appear in the *Bhismaparvan* section of the *Māhabhārata*.[2] Radhakrishnan refers to the controversy among the scholars concerning the connection between the *Gita* and the *Māhabhārata*. Some scholars argue that Krsna could not have recited the entire text of the *Gita* containing seven hundred verses to Arjuna, just before the battle of Kurukshetra began. But when we consider the fact that *Māhabhārata* is full of many miraculous events, this argument does not suffice to show that the *Gita* must predate the writing of the epic by Vyasa or whoever the original author was. Nevertheless Garbe maintains that the *Gita* was originally a *Sāṁkhya-yoga* treatise of the theistic cult Vasudevism. Hopkins, Holtzmann, Keith, Barnett, and Otto are all quoted by Radhakrishnan as believers in the idea that the *Gita's* original composition predates *Māhabhārata* and it might have been a late *Upanishad* and certainly a text of the Kṛṣṇaite and Vishnuite theistic sects, later worked over by some exponent of *Vedānta*.[3] It is no surprise that early indologists who regard the *Gita* as primarily and fundamentally a theistic text which, according to them, proclaims a theistic revolution in Indian thought, would trace its origins in the earliest theistic cults such as Vasudevism, Pañcharātra, as well as in classical Vaisnavism.

Among the contemporary scholars, Zaehner who also has a predominently theistic interpretation of the *Gita*, and believes that "it is Ramanuja who probably comes nearest to the mind of the author of the *Gita*," nevertheless maintains that "the *Gita* was originally conceived as an integral part of the Epic." Zaehner points toward Book fourteen of the epic where Kṛṣṇa plays the role of Arjuna's teacher once again in the so-called *Anugita* or Gita Recapitulated, which is not a comprehensive recapitulation for it omits the "mysterious" parts dealing with the love of God. The *Gita* is

> Spoken by the Lord incarnate at the most solemn moment of the whole enormous story, the moment to which everything else has been working up . . . the moment when a just retribution will overwhelm God's enemies.[4]

THE PROBLEMS OF A GENERAL INTERPRETATION OF THE *GITA*

The issue of the *Gita's* connection with the epic *Māhabhārata* has important implications for the history of the idea of bhakti in the traditions of Indian thought. Several scholars believe that the *Gita* is not only a watershed in the march of bhakti but also the very reservoir of bhakti or "theistic" religious movements with Hinduism. Although the author of the *Gita* presents a harmonious account of *Sāṁkhya*, *Yoga*, *Vedanta* as well as the theistic cult of *Vasudevism*, it is a general tendency of the various theistic interpreters to either polarize the *Vedānta* and non-*Vedānta* elements in the *Gita*, or downplay the *Vedānta*, i.e., Upanishadic ingredients of the *Gita's* own system of thought. Bhakti is viewed as largely absent in the pre-*Bhagavadgita* texts such as the *Vedas*, *Upanishads*, and the *Brahma Sutras*, as well as missing in the religious beliefs of the people of the age of *Vedas* and *Upanishads* with the exception of some theistic cults of Vāsudeva and Kṛṣṇa worshippers of the age immediately preceding the composition of the *Māhabhārata*.

The modern interpreters of the *Gita* beginning with the early indologists, including contemporary scholars of religious studies and of Indian philosophy show some peculiar proclivities, some common biases rooted in the very origin of indological studies even though each one of them has made individual contributions toward scholarship on the *Gita*. The modern interpreters have created and fallen prey to various dichotomies in their terminologies. A grand dichotomy is established between philosophy and religion. Radhakrishnan begins his introduction to his *Gita* translation with the statement: "The *Bhagavadgita* is more a religious classic than a philosophical treatise."[5] If this is stated to emphasize that *Gita* offers guidelines to live well rather than mere arguments, it may be fair. Otherwise, it is hardly justified to call a treatise that offers a fundamental analysis of the connection between action, knowledge, and love not strictly "philosophical." In any case, many modern *Gita* interpreters often show a tendency to dismiss the *Vedānta* and metaphysical aspects of the text as mere philosophy, and regard its theistic elements as essential and religious. This is why some early indologists even undertook to cleanse the *Gita* of its extra-Godly elements by creating an *Ur-Gita*. In this connection Zehner's remarks are on the mark:

> The bulk of the poem is not concerned with the respective merits of war and peace, but with the deepest things of man and God. No wonder then that German scholars have sought to dig out an original *Gita* from under what they consider to be a mass of strictly irrelevant metaphysics. No wonder that others have tried to treat the *Gita* as a separate poem that somehow or other got itself inserted into the great Epic.[6]

Another dichotomy that is widely invoked is that of monism versus monotheism. Thought and worship of the age of the *Vedas* is described as polytheistic, creating an impression that monism and theism were absent in it. The *Upanishads* are taken as replete with monism, offering a systematic account of the grand equation between *ātman* and *Brahman*. The *Gita* is almost universally acclaimed as the first systematic proclamation of monotheism, combined with a religionization of bhakti. Things would be much simpler if all these basically Western concepts could neatly explain the evolution of Vedic thought. Unfortunately, things are much more complex and these categories forbid us to realize how polytheism, monism, and monotheism coexist within all these historical periods and within all these seminal texts. As we will demonstrate in this chapter, monism and theism certainly coexist in the

Gita, and bhakti has not left its secular sense of love behind by transferring itself into a purely religious meaning as the bond between man and God. Here a mere etymological analysis of the kind that Dhavamony has done does not reveal the fuller implications of bhakti.[7] The evolving relation between Arjuna and the Bhāgavat, from friendship, to discipleship (*guru-şişya*) to the devotion toward God, indicates that bhakti is the soul of love, secular or religious, and all these meanings of love are explored and established in the *Gita*. Furthermore, the Upanishadic insight is neither abandoned, nor transformed but rather pressed into service of a harmonious summary of the Hindu concepts offered by the *Gita*, which includes a theism that does not oppose monism, but is reconciled with it.

Thus it is the composite nature of the text that compounds the difficulties of a fair interpretation. Besides offering a summation of the well-established systems of *Vedānta*, *Sāṁkhya*, *Yoga*, and the preceding theistic sects, the *Gita* also makes numerous references to other sects, gods, sages, seers, poets, and ascetics. It presents a picture of religious and philosophical pluralism of the times. Even though by and large the modern interpreters have exaggerated the theistic aspects of the *Gita*, it remains one of the standard sourcebooks of monism and nondualistic *Vedānta* systems. In fact, all the six systems of Hindu thought acknowledge the *Gita* as an authoritative text. It is not confined to be the leading light of theistic sects and schools of Hinduism, but remains a basic and popular text of all the various brands and thought-systems of Hinduism. It is a text that was written to simplify, and succinctly summarize the essence of Hinduism or in other words, of *Vedānta* for the masses. Even though its original version was written in Sanskrit, it has been popular as a Hindu bible for the ordinary believers. It has also come to be a standard, concise introduction to Hinduism and its essential systems for non-Hindus. It remains one of the most important texts of philosophy of all time for it raises fundamental ontological, epistemological, and ethical issues. In the words of Hiriyanna,

> Its author, as may be expected from one whom tradition reckons as the inspirer of practically all Sanskrit poets, does not discuss here the subtle and recondite details of ethics and metaphysics, but deals only with the broad principles underlying them, relating them at the same time to the most fundamental aspirations of man. . . .
>
> All this, however, does not mean that the work is easy of understanding. Far from it. It is one of the hardest books to interpret, which accounts for the numerous commentaries on it—each differing from the rest in some essential point or the other.[8]

The fusion of various systems within a single text makes it a compendium of ideas and makes accessible to the reader numerous possibilities of thought. The classical commentators, especially the exponents of the various subschools of *Vedānta*, such as Sankara (788–820 A.D.), Ramanuja (1017–1137 A.D.), Madhava (1199–1276), Nimbarka (1162 A.D.), and Vallabha (1479 A.D.) wrote their celebrated accounts of the *Gita*. These commentaries were written in a way to justify and validate their respective systems of *Vedānta*. They were followed by classical commentaries by scholars within their own schools. Although there are references made to some commentators preceding Sankara, their works are not extant. The fact that several modern commentators have a tendency to latch on to one or the other of these classical commentators compounds the problem of interpreting the *Gita*. Zaehner identifies the problem and suggests a remedy, the full implications of which he himself fails to follow by strongly endorsing Ramanuja's theistic interpretation:

> In interpreting the *Gita*, as in interpreting any sacred text (or indeed any text) the danger is that the interpreter will quote all that is grist to his mill while failing to draw attention to what embarrasses him in other parts of the text. . . . As far as the ancient commentators (Sankara and Ramanuja) are concerned, I have confined myself on the whole to their interpretation of individual words and phrases, since in their philosophical commentaries they invariably read their own philosophical and theological views into the text.[9]

Obviously, it is hard for any interpreter not to be selective, especially if the account is obliged to be brief. At the same time, one's project can easily turn into an agenda. However, we must acknowledge that while the *Gita* offers some original insights in an original manner, it is at the same time an interpretative text of its own past. Thus numerous systems and points of view are reconciled in it and their mutual contradictions are underemphasized. In our interpretation, while we want to re-emphasize the *advaita* (nondual) and *nirguna* (attributelessness) aspects of ultimate reality within the *Gita*, which is often downplayed and even ignored by the passionately theistic interpreters, we do not want to deny that *Gita* is a theistic text as well. A fuller account of its theism must include the *advaita* and *nirguna* aspects of the ultimate Being and not only its personal attributes. This has important implications for the meaning of bhakti. It is not to be taken merely as devotion of a personal god but a *yoga* of *karma*, in the sense of self-transformation, *jñāna*, in the sense knowing what is worth knowing and Being, and bhakti in the sense of realizing that to be is to devote oneself selflessly.

THE ROLE OF BHAKTI IN THE *GITA*: SOME PROBLEMS

In most of the modern interpretations of the *Gita*, the role of bhakti is exaggerated to claim that the *Gita* is the first authentic enunciation of theism within Hinduism. At the same time the notion of bhakti is woefully narrowed down, detached from its companion concept of *jñāna*, severed from its own history within Indian thought, and viewed in isolation from its human context, in its specific incarnation as the "Hindu devotion." This amounts to a misinterpretation that may perhaps be redeemed by a new look at the history of interpretations, old and new of the *Gita*. We should also keep in mind that just because Hinduism has used the method of love and devotion creatively in its religious and philosophical quest, it does not make love and devotion exclusively "Hindu" or even exclusively "religious." *Prema* (love) and bhakti are human activities, human tendencies, and human emotions. These were invited into the religious and philosophical domains by all major religious traditions, such as Hinduism, Buddhism, Jainism, Sikhism, as well as by numerous philosophical traditions, schools of thought, sects and cults, either associated or not associated with the above-named religious traditions. It is true that some texts, schools, and sects are more bhakti oriented than others. That does not mean that bhakti is confined to these and absent from the rest. Nor does it mean that a split is to be made within Hinduism to recognize something called "Bhakti Hinduism" as distinct from the so-called Brahmanism. To group Vaisnavism, Saivism, and the bhakti saints of the bhakti movement as detached from Brahmanism and from the quest for *jñāna* is to misunderstand them.

Is the *Gita* a poetic summary of Hindu thought as it stood in the times of its composition or is it a radically new thesis on the nature of the Absolute? Is *Gita* a rehash of the previous systems or marked by its own new system of thought? These questions obviously allude to extreme positions. It is clear to a serious reader that the *Gita* has both the old and the new. However, these issues are intertwined with the definition and treatment of bhakti within the text and how this role of bhakti vis-à-vis *jñāna* and *karma* has been interpreted by the modern scholars. Krishna Sharma in her valuable book *Bhakti and Bhakti Movement*, describes the theistically biased interpretations of some modern scholars, as follows:

> It was in the course of the modern theorization on bhakti that the *Bhagavadgita* was projected as the earliest literary exposition of the "Bhakti religion." Lorinser was the first to describe the *Gita* as that. This assessment of the *Gita* was not questioned thereafter in discussions on the bhakti theme. The *Gita* therefore is invariably treated as a *Vaisnava* text in them—and also as a theistic Hindu scripture which concentrated upon a personal concept of God. Taking it as "an expression of the earliest attempt made in India to rise to a theistic faith and theology" (Farquhar, p. 86) and as "a vindication of a popular religion of the Bhagvatas" independent of the Vedic tradition (Grierson; pp. 539–51; Garbe, pp. 535–38), its mono-theism is explained as a stage different from the pantheism of

the Upanishads. Supported by such arguments the *Gita* is considered unique among the Hindu scriptures for its notion of bhakti which is particularized and regarded as "almost a new note in Hindu speculation." (Edgerton, p. 71)[10]

In several theistic interpretations of the *Gita*, by early indologists and scholars of religious studies, the transcendence of the Kṛṣṇa figure, who is either absent or shown as an ordinary mortal in other parts of the *Mahābhārata*, is interpreted as a transformation of the *Brahman* of the *Upanishads* into a personal God. It is also seen as the exaltation of the path (*marga*) of bhakti as an alternative to the path of *jñāna*, an easier alternative open to people from all castes and both genders and not merely to scholars and pundits. It is claimed in this regard that the main source for *Gita's* theism is not the *Vedas*, *Upanishads*, and the *Brahma Sutras*, but the popular *Vaisnava* cult of *Bhāgavatas* who were already worshipping Kṛṣṇa-Vāsudeva, and according to some theories, were the offshoot of a very ancient tradition that ran parallel to Vedic tradition. Thus a long-standing split existed between the elitist, scholarly, philosophical, *jñāna*-oriented *Brahmanism* and the popular, theistic, bhakti-oriented faith of the masses. This artificial splitting of Hinduism into two parts, the separation of theory from practice, and of bhakti from *jñāna* is unacceptable to some contemporary scholars like Krishna Sharma. It seems that the *Gita* scholarship is puzzled about the relation between *Brahman* invoked in the *Upanishads*, and the dynamic and self-evolving Kṛṣṇa figure of the *Gita*, who was the God of the *Bhāgavatas*, a character in the *Mahābhārata* and Arjuna's friend, guru, and God all rolled into one. Sometimes he is a gentle guide, sometimes a charioteer of our fate. He is sometimes an *avatāra*, i.e. god come hither and sometimes shows his *viṣva-rūpa* (universal form), sometimes embodied and sometimes attributeless. His *Brahman* aspects are emphasized rather than undervalued in the text. Thus the relation between Krsna and *Brahman* needs to be rethought for it continues to be a challenging problem for a serious reader of this valuable and richly philosophical text.

As Krishna Sharma points out, the *Gita's* connection with the *Upanishads* was acknowledged by early Hindu theologians like Sankara, Ramanuja, Madhava, Vallabha, and Nimbarka, whether or not they had a theistic interpretation of the text on the whole.[11] That the *Gita* offers a synthesis especially of *Yoga*, *Sāṁkhya*, and *Vedānta* schools is acknowledged by the modern scholars as well. But this composite nature of the *Gita* is "conveniently ignored in all academic discussions on bhakti where *Gita* is treated as a purely *Vaisnava* text and as a scripture formulated by the *Bhāgavatas*."[12]

This also means, as we shall show in our exposition below, that the *yoga* of *karma, bhakti*, and *jñāna* is misunderstood, as bhakti is detached from the other two existential factors, and exaggerated to be nothing but "theistic devotion" which is a limited view of bhakti that the *Gita* does not really propound. What the *Gita* advocates is that in an ideal human existence, action, love, and knowledge are to be allowed to dwell in the vicinity of each other. Each is to be viewed in terms of the other. One is to act devotedly and in the know of *Brahman*; one is to devote oneself, actively and in terms of the knowledge of God; and one is to seek to know, devotedly and actively. "Be thou the *yogin*, Arjuna," "Remember me and fight." Kṛṣṇa calls for a fusion of action, bhakti, and knowledge. He does not ask for a mere surrender to himself, or for a blind, effortless, and submissive devotion to God.

The title of the work literally means "The Song of the *Bhagavad*." The words *Bhagavad* or *Bhāgavat* are the synonyms of the term "*Bhagavān*," which is used for a deity or for the highest spiritual masters. Both the Buddha and the Mahavira were addressed as *Bhagavān*, as were Kṛṣṇa and Rama, the deified heroes of the epics *Mahābhārata* and *Rāmāyana*. Brahma, Visna, and Siva, the Hindu trinity of highest gods are also given the title *Bhagavān*. In the later ages and in the modern times, the devotees occasionally apply the title to their spiritual masters, e.g., Sai Baba, the living saint from South India is being called *Bhagavān* by his followers. Within the *Gita*, whenever Kṛṣṇa speaks, the author uses the phrase "*sri bhagvān uvāca* (spoke)" but whenever Arjuna speaks, it is merely mentioned as "Arjuna *uvacha*." *Bhagavān* is the most commonly used term for "God" for all Hindus. The word "gita" means the song, indicating that the work is a poetical composition (comprised of seven hundred stanzas) and is meant to be a grand hymn on the nature of God. That explains why the *Gita* summarizes, synthesizes, and harmonizes philosophical concepts, arguments, and insights in a work that seems to be written for the masses rather than for the scholars and pundits alone. Its stanzas are easily committed to memory and widely quoted due primarily to their poetic style and practical relevance. Thus the use of the term song (*gita*) in the title means that it is not meant to be unduly tedious, dry, hermeneutically challenging, or overly scholastic work. Compared to it the *Upanishads* and *Brahama Sutras*, the other texts of the *prasthāntryi* (the triad of authoritative texts) or even other *srūti* (revealed) texts are much more dense and require scholarly aids for interpretation. The *Gita*, in terms of its structure and content, is way more concise, uncomplicated, and self-contained.

The term *Bhagavād* may be indicative of the *Gita's* connection with the theistic sect of the *bhagavātas* who are known to have addressed their deity as *sri bhagavān*. The word *bhagavān* literally means one who possesses *bhāga*, that is fortune, wealth, blessings; hence its usual translation the "Blessed One." The term *bhāga* also means "portion," and thus *bhagavān* also means one who allocates proper portion or fate of each creature. *Bhagavān* is thus the grand disposer of one's fate, wealth, and blessings. This sense is conveyed by the popular adage "man proposes, God disposes." In the history of Indian theism, the sects of *bhāgavatas* and Pañchrātras are cited as the earliest practitioners of theistic bhakti. The term *bhāgavata* means one who belongs to the *bhāgavat* or a *bhāgavat*-worshipper. The *bhāgavatas* worshipped a deity called Narayana, a name of Visnu, which was later called Vāsudeva, a name also given to Kṛṣṇa. According to a theory, the *bhāgavata* cult may be traceable way back into the Indus Valley civilization, and is non-Vedic, i.e., independent of the Upanishadic thought, although it adopted some Vedic ideas. The cult is mentioned in the *Mahābhārata* and was thriving in the times of the Gupta dynasty (fourth to sixth century) and also mentioned in the *Purānas* (religious histories), especially in the *Bhāgavat-Purāna* (tenth century). Pañchrātra was another *Vaisnava* sect of Vāsudeva-worshippers that is not connected with the *Gita* but is mentioned in other documents, especially *Pañcharātra-samhita*, quoted by Ramanuja in his commentary on *Brahma Sutra*[13] and other *saṁhitas* (collections) such as *satvata-saṁhita*. This sect is also cited as practicing religious bhakti and having resistance toward Vedic values and the caste system.

As the research work of R. G. Bhandarkar indicates, the deity of Vāsudeva-Kṛṣṇa, the *Bhāgavat* was identified with Narayana and Visnu on the one hand and amalgamated with that of Gopāla-Kṛṣṇa (cowherd god) a few centuries later. Thus the incarnated lord that appears in the *Gita* is an amalgamation of several previously acknowledged deities.

> Vāsudeva could not have been living when the *Bhagavadgita* was composed as a discourse delivered by him, any more than Buddha was living when his discourses were reduced to the form of books. It is worthy of remark that both of them are called *Bhagvats* when speaking. Vāsudeva must have already been deified before the *Bhagavadgita* was written.[14]

The historicity of Kṛṣṇa is a debatable issue. Some people who regard *Mahābhārata* and *Rāmāyana* as mythological sagas, consider their characters by and large fictitious. However, several individuals, clans, places, and events mentioned in the epics sporadically turn out to be historical facts. Modern historians rely on the information given in *Vedas*, *Upanishads* and the epics as well as other documents of the religious lore to reconstruct the social life and political conditions in various periods of history. In the introduction of his translation of the *Bhagavadgita*, Radhakrishnan traces the historicity of the Kṛṣṇa figure as follows after he cautions that the whole issue has nothing to do with the value of the message contained in the work:

> There is however ample evidence in favour of the historicity of Kṛṣṇa. The *Chandyoga Upanishad* refers to Kṛṣṇa, devakiputra, the son of *Devaki*, and speaks of him as the pupil of Ghora Angirasa. . . . Kṛṣṇa plays an important part

> in the story of the Mahābhārata where he is presented as the friend of Arjuna. Panini (fifth century B.C.) refers to Vāsudeva and Arjuna as objects of worship. Kṛṣṇa belonged to the ancient Vrsni or Satvata branch of the family of Yadu (Yadavas are a community or caste of agriculturists in modern India). In *Mahabharatha*, Krsna is represnted both as an historical individual and as an incarnation (*avatāra*). . . .
>
> By the fourth century before Christ, the cult of Vāsudeva was well-established. In the Buddhist work Niddesa (fourth century B.C.) included in the Pali canon, the writer refers to the worshippers of Vāsudeva and Baladeva. . . . Magasthenes (320 B.C.) states that Haracles (Hari) was worshipped by the *sourasenoi (surasenas)* . . . Heliodorous, the Greek *Bhagavata* from Texila, calls Vāsudeva, *devadeva* (god of gods) in the Besanager inscription (180 B.C.). The Nanaghat inscription (first century B.C.) mentioned Vāsudeva among the deities invoked . . . Radha, Yasoda, and Nanda (Krsna's associates) figure in Buddhist legends. Patanjali (second century B.C.), commenting on Panini (IV, 3. 98) calls Vāsudeva, *Bhagvat*.[15]

Thus the author of the *Gita* seems to have chosen an already recognized incarnation of Visnu, who will reveal to the innocent, for the word *arjuna* literally means "innocent" or "guileless," his own nature, including the relation of the *Isvara* (personal God, object of bhakti) to *Brahman* or *Puruṣa* of the *Vedas*. It is better, he might have thought, that a fundamental discourse on the nature of God and man, be in the form of a dialogue between *Bhāgavat* the God and Arjuna, the man. The dialogue form, often used by ancient philosophers, both eastern (e.g., parts of the *Upanishads*) and western (e.g., Plato), to make tedious arguments and analyses of otherwise obtuse subject matter more interesting and humane. For it is more impressive for God to appear as an interlocutor and say "I am thus and thus" than having to read a scholastic essay on God's attributes in the third person. The poetic and dramatic features of the *Gita* are obvious. It is a work in which both the characters Arjuna and Krsna reveal their evolving personalities and status. In the unfolding mysteries of the respective Beings of man and God, the possibilities of the human entity and of the knowledge of the divine are elucidated with the authoritative stamp of Indian thought with no violence to its pluralistic character.

BHAKTI AND THE GITA: CHAPTERS 1–6

Chapter 1 of the *Gita* provides us with a context for the teachings to be imparted to Arjuna, the human being by Kṛṣṇa, the God come hither, the *nirguṇa* (attributeless) become *saguṇa* (attributed). The teachings consist of the basic issues concerning action, devotion, and knowledge that affect the human entity, together with a succinct summary of the Vedic worldview. The first chapter links the body of the religio-philosphical discourse with the story of the epic *Mahābhārata* of which the *Gita* is an integral part. At the same time, the predicament of Arjuna, the warrior at the moment of the commencement of the battle is symbolic of the basic human vacillation on whether or not to fight the tendencies of worldly attachment (*moha*) and sloth (*tamas*) to perform one's calling (*svā-dharma*) with enthusiasm. That Kuruksetra, the locale of the battle, is a *dharma-ksetra* mentioned by the Blind King Dhrtarastra, when he asks the narrator Samjaya about what transpired just before the hostilities began (I-1). Human life is a field of *dharma*, an arena of moral struggle where right or wrong, desirable or undesirable have yet to be determined, and the framework of reasoning behind this determination has yet to be understood. Moral confusion and hesitancy is not merely Arjuna's problem, it is a universal state of affairs. Moral do's and don'ts do not come to us in ready-made packages. Principles and theories have to be applied to specific situations. Just as for Arjuna, to fight or not to fight (*moha, mamtā,* and *māyā*) is a question for all human beings.

The *Gita* begins with a description of how Arjuna becomes despondent when he is face to face with a throng of kinsmen, revered teachers, and friends, whom he must fight and slay in order to be victorious in this war. Being a warrior and a master of archery, Arjuna had killed many a foe in his career, but this is a strange situation. This time he must kill those he loves and reveres, those with whom he has bonds of *mamtā*. Love of the near and dear prevents him from doing his *dharma*, makes him question his *dharma*. Vinoba Bhave cites an example to illustrate Arjuna's predicament.[16] Once upon a time a judge who had sent a number of criminals to the death suddenly had his own son in his court accused of murder. The judge now had a change of heart; he began to entertain arguments in mind that the death penalty is truly barbaric and ought to be abolished. The thoughts going through Arjuna's mind just before the start of the battle are similar to the thoughts suddenly dawning upon the mind of the judge who must send his own son to the gallows in the name of justice. Arjuna has had no qualms about being a warrior and killing whoever he had to all his life long. But in this battleground of Kuruksetra things are different; this time he has to annihilate his kinsfolk toward whom he has the rush of *mamtā* (mine-ness). And it is this *mamtā* that urges him to become a nonviolent man and even give up his *svā-dharma* and adopt the vocation of a *sanyāsi* (ascetic).

The first chapter also suggests that the purpose of the sermon to the warrior by the incarnated Lord is nothing as simple as reminding him of his "caste duty" and convincing him to lead the army to victory. One of the major issues discussed in this song of the *Bhāgavat*, is that of *svā-dharma* (self-*dharma*, one's vocation, one's calling, one's attitude to action) which is not the same thing as the *jāti-dharma* (*caste dharma*) or *varna-dharma.* If *svā-dharma* meant merely *varṇa dharma*, Kṛṣṇa's advice could have been quite simple: all must follow their respective caste-duties, therefore Arjuna must be a warrior as best he can. Instead the issue of *svā-dharma* as an individual's very own problem, to act or not to act as well as how to act meritoriously, is discussed at length in the *Gita*, which may be called a treatise on the nature and significance of human action (*karma*). In any case, the introductory first chapter of the *Gita* shows Arjuna (literally: innocent, guileless) in the grip of a mistaken and illusory bhakti toward his kin, which is nothing but *mamtā* and *moha*. His thinking is clouded by the mist of attachments, and bhakti toward *svā-dharma* and toward God is far from his mind.

The colophon at the end of the first chapter of the *Gita* indicates this text's intimate connection with the body of the Vedic texts. It is called an *Upanishad* in its own right and an exposition of the science of *Brahman* (*brahmavidyāyam*) as well as a scripture of yoga (*yogasāṣtre*). This declaration should refute the theories which posit the *Gita* as the beginning of new "bhakti religion" radically different in spirit from the Vedic and Upanishadic contemplation of the *nirguṇa Brahman*. The colophon is worded as follows:

> In the Upanishad of the *Bhagavadgita*, the science of *brahman*, the scripture of yoga and the dialogue between sri kṛṣṇa and Arjuna, this is the first chapter entitled the Depression of Arjuna.

The second chapter of the *Gita* provides an introduction to the content of the text and offers a synopsis of the issues discussed in this short treatise. It offers both the theory of *Sāṁkhya* and the practice of *yoga*. The terms *Sāṁkhya* and *yoga* herein do not stand for the Hindu systems of thought under the same titles. Vinoba Bhave explains it very well:

> The *Gita* has a way of using old philosophical terms in new senses. These principles enunciated in the *Gita* are found already in the *Upanishads* and *Smṛtis*. If the *Gita* merely repeated them, it would be no great distinction. Its real merit is that it tells us how to bring these truths into practice.
>
> *Yoga* is the name of the art or process by which these principles can be put into practice in the actual living. The word *Sāṁkhya* means principles or theory. *Yoga* means art or well-doing . . . The *Gita* is full of both, *Sāṁkhya* and *yoga*, science and art, *sāstra* and *kalā*.[17]

Gita will have a lot to expound on the issue of *yoga*, the art of unification of disparate strands of theoretical knowledge that one carries in one's head after being convinced of their truth. It is an art of living according to one's valued and cherished beliefs received through authority, tradition, and for personal conviction. Standing on the horns of dilemma, overwhelmed by his cloudy vision, shaken by self-pity and deep depression, Arjuna seeks refuge from Kṛṣṇa whom he places on the pedestal of the guru. He implores his friend to become his guru; he requests his charioteer to be his spiritual charioteer. The *Bhāgavat*, the grand charioteer of the lives of all on this earth, will respond to Arjuna's bhakti. Arjuna graphically describes his physical and psychological condition to the guru:

> My being is stricken with the weakness of sentimental pity. With my mind bewildered about my duty, I ask Thee. Tell me for certain, which is better. I am thy pupil (*şişya*); teach me, who am taking refuge in thee. (II-7)

After this change in the dynamic relationship between the two interlocutors, as their personal love grows into *guru-bhakti*, Arjuna is given some fundamental knowledge concerning the eternal element in human entity. This spirit or *ātman* in us is deathless. Thus there is no utter annihilation of anybody, including those relatives and teachers who might perish in the Kurukstra war. Passages II-20 and II-29 contain direct quotations from the *Katha Upanishad* (18 and 7) on the nature of *ātman*: "It is not slain, when the body is slain" and

> One looks upon it as a marvel, another likewise speaks of it as a marvel, another hears of it as a marvel; and even after hearing, no one whatsoever has known it. (II-29)

No one has comprehended the Self absolutely. Being the most wonderful enigma of human life, the quest for it must continue. The second most important instruction by the *Bhāgavat* for his pupil has to do with *svā-dharma*, which must not be ignored. Since Arjuna's *svā-dharma* is being a warrior he must fight a battle "enjoined by duty" (II-31). The more fundamental message is that one must fight the tendencies in oneself as well as circumstances in the external world that deter or distract oneself from one's *svā-dharma*. *Svā-dharma* is something to fight for, something to be sought in the *dharma ksetra* (arena of dharma) that is life. Regarding action within one's *svā-dharma*, Arjuna (i.e., mankind) is given the golden rule:

> To action alone hast thou a right and never at all to its fruits; let not the fruits of action be thy motive, neither let there be in thee any attachment to inaction. (II-47)
>
> Fixed in *yoga* do thy work, O winner of wealth (Arjuna), abandoning attachment, with an even mind in success and failure, for evenness of mind is called *yoga*. (II-48)

Thus *svā-dharma* is to be performed but not with an eye on the fruit. "Let not the fruits of action be thy motive." The devotion to *svā-dharma* makes duty a spontaneous and natural affair. *Gita* forbids attachment to inactivity. *Yoga* means action, so vital, and so natural to all human beings. "Fixed in *yoga* do thy work" implies that knowledge, action, and bhakti are to be fused together, their *yoga* (union) makes one's work something spontaneous, lovable, and devotional rather than a drudgery or a burdensome affair. Work becomes worship and its own reward when *karma* and bhakti are intertwined.

> Do thou thy allotted work, for action is better than inaction, even the maintenance of thy physical life cannot be affected without action. (III-8)
>
> Better is one's own law (*svadharma*) though imperfectly carried out than the law of another (*para-dharma*) carried out perfectly. Better is death in (the fulfillment of) ones own law for to follow another's law is perilous. (III-35)

One's allotted work that emerges out of one's vocation, calling, and station, is the field in which one must remain active. But this is not to be done for a specific outcome, reward, or profit, or with selfish motives. Bhakti for the *svā-dharma* and a bhakti-laden performance makes human life worthwhile. Action with sacrifice (*karma* as *yajna*), i.e., action that gives up the fruit is the best form of action, the natural approach of the true leaders of society for "whatsoever a great man does, the same is done by others as well. Whatever standard he sets, the world follows" (III-21). A superior person (*srestha*) excels in the performance of his or her *svā-dharma*, and does so without a selfish agenda, by invoking bhakti in the heart of karma. For this devoted individual knows that better is *svā-dharma* even though imperfectly carried out, that is, even though it fails to show spectacular profit or success. It is better to die in the process of its performance than to be a cog in somebody else's machine, to be a slave to other people's agendas. For work done in alienation to one's own creativity, that Karl Marx called "alienation of labour" is sheer drudgery, a far cry from *svā-dharma*. The *Bhāgavat* profoundly remarks that even the journey of the body (*sarirayatra*); or the maintenance of the physical life cannot continue without action. But action in the domain of *svā-dharma* is the best.

> This same ancient *yoga* has been today declared to thee by me; for thou art my devotee (*bhakta*) and my friend (*sakha*); and this is the supreme secret. (IV-3)
>
> Whenever there is decline of *dharma* and rise of *adharma*, O Bharata (Arjuna), then I send forth myself. (IV-7)

The *jñāna-yoga* being transmitted to Arjuna is ancient but exclusive knowledge that the *Bhāgavat* is imparting out of love to his special friend and devotee. Here friendship and bhakti, secular love, and religious devotion are spoken of in the same breath. The friend become devotee is still a friend; the devotional love is modeled on the human love. But whenever there is a decline of *dharma*, the *Bhāgavat* incarnates himself sends forth himself (*avatāra*) in human form, out of love for mankind. This is a two-way love; humans love God; God loves and cares for mankind. It is not an abstract love but love for an individual, conceived in this Vedic tradition on the model of love between persons.

> He who works, having given up attachment, resigning his actions to God (*Brahman*), is not touched by sin, even as a lotus (is untouched) by water. (V-10)
>
> Thinking of that, directing one's whole conscious being to that, making that their whole aim, with that as the sole object of devotion, they reach a state from which there is no return, their sins washed away with wisdom. (V-17)

The *karma-yogi* who performs action within his *svā-dharma* selflessly, in a way devotes his work to something other and higher than himself, to *Brahman*, translated here in many other passages as "God" by Radhakrishnan and other scholars in their attempt to make the *Gita* ever more theistic than it is. Whereas there are some references to personal God in the *Gita*, there are also numerous others to *nirguṇa Brahman*, for instance the author of the *Gita* chooses to call the ultimate divine Being just "That" in the above passage. The point here is, however, that the unselfish performance of duty is steadier when the work that is already a devotion to *svā-dharma* becomes part of one's devotion to God, to that ultimate divine Being. The fruit, the outcome, and the reward of the work is also left up to God. The outcome of the work is submitted to his will. This way of devotion and sacrifice are built into one's creative work and an unselfish and dedicated performance gets underway.

> What they call renunciation (*sanyāsa*) that know to be disciplined activity, O Pandava (Arjuna), for no one becomes a *yogin* who has not renounced his (selfish) purpose. (VI-2)
>
> He who sees me everywhere and sees all in me; I am not lost to him nor is he lost to me. (VI-30)
>
> And of all *yogins*, he who is full of faith (*sraddha*) worships (*bhajate*) me with his inner self abiding in me, him I hold to be the most attuned (to me in *yoga*). (VI-47)

The *Gita* outlines the character of a true *yogin* who has carried an attitude of renunciation into his creative activity by giving up his selfish purpose and dedicating his work and its outcomes to the *Bhāgavat*. The God conceived here is no different from what the *Upanishads* refer to as *Brahman*, whom the *yogin* sees all around, dwelling in all beings. The *Bhāgavat* is never far from the mind of a yogin and such a one receives God's constant love and attention. Out of all devotees full of *bhakti* and *sraddhā* one who loves and knows *Brahman* personally "with his inner self abiding in me," i.e., knows his *ātman* as rooted in *Brahman*, is dearmost to *Bhāgavat* and regarded as a perfect *yogin*. In other words, devoted activity (*karma* and *bhakti*) alone does not make a perfect *yogin*. Knowledge (*jñāna*) of Brahman is also required for a perfect practice of *yoga*.

BHAKTI AND THE *GITA*, CHAPTERS 7–12

In the first six chapters of the *Gita* the *karma-yoga*, the action, the necessity of action, and the various aspects of action are elucidated. This is done so of course by tracing the connection of human action with *svā-dharma*, *akarma* (nonaction), *sanyāsa* (renunciation), and a host of other implications. The next six chapters, *bhakti-yoga* is presented and the last six chapters are devoted to the *jñāna-yoga*. The three themes of *karma, bhakti*, and *jñāna* are not exposed in three watertight compartments, but the interconnections and unity (*yoga*) are discussed in various parts of the texts. In the seventh chapter, the floodgates of bhakti seem to be thrown open. Bhakti is presented as an effective means to know *Isvara* (God). It is emphasized that love is a genuine means to get closer to and know God, and without the involvement of the heart, both action and knowledge remain limited and held back from their fuller possibilities.

> This divine *māyā* of mine, consisting of the modes is hard to overcome. But those who take refuge in me alone cross beyond it. (VII-14)

The spell of *māyā* (illusory worldliness) is hard to cross over. Mere knowledge and self-control are not sufficient to traverse the internal cravings (*kāmā*), attachments (*moha*), and temptations of the world. Taking a love-driven refuge in something higher, the refuge in the grace of the *Bhāgavat*, produces in us true indifference to the temptations of the world and makes us ready for a devoted performance of *svā-dharma*.

> The virtuous ones who worship me are of four kinds; the man in distress, the seeker after knowledge, the seeker for wealth and the man of wisdom, O Lord of the Bhāratas (Arjuna). (VII-16)
>
> Of these the wise one, who is ever in constant union with the divine, whose devotion is single-minded, is the best. For I am supremely dear to him and he is dear to me. (VII-17)

The text says that of those performers of good deeds (*sukṛtināh*) who worship (*bhajante*) the *Bhāgavat*, there are four types: the afflicted (*artah*), the seeker of knowledge (*jijñāsuh*), the seeker of worldly ends (*artharthi*), and the man of knowledge (*jñāni*). Of these the *jñāni*, endowed with steadfastness (*nitya-yaktah*), with single one-pointed bhakti (*eka-bhaktih*) surpasses others. The first three devotees seek something for themselves, whereas the fourth one, the *jñāni* is a disinterested seer who submits himself to the highest Being, fully realizing that *Brahman* dwells in everything. To such a *jñāni*, *Bhāgavat* is the dearest (*priya*), and he is dear to the *Bhāgavat*. The love of such a perfect practitioner of love is reciprocated. The *jñāni* has achieved the union of *karma*, *bhakti*, and *jñāna* in his one-pointed submission the *Bhāgavat*. He knows all entities as pervaded by *Brahman* and acts accordingly and devotes himself accordingly. It is noteworthy that there is no dichotomy between the notion of *Brahman* and that of *Bhāgavat*, nor are bhakti and *jñāna* posited as distinct activities. Their fusion and acting dutifully but spontaneously according to this unity is what is warranted. True bhakti is nothing other than *jñāna* but inclusive of *jñāna.*

The act of bhakti is given great importance by the *Gita*. Even seekers of their personal ends, the first three types of *bhaktas*, the afflicted, the knowledge seekers, the seekers of worldliness (*artha*) are all called doers of good (*sukṛtina*). Those "who resort to other gods," and "devotees with faith (of any kind)" (VII-20, 21) are not called ignorant but even their reverence is indirectly reaching out to *Bhāgavat*, for after all, their deities are the forms of the divine. But

> Men of no understanding think of one, the unmanifest as having manifestation, not knowing my higher nature, changeless and supreme. (VII-24)

Those still bereft of *jñāna*, regard the forms of other gods or even the supreme Being in terms of attributes. They don't still realize that *Brahman* abides in all these forms that are subject to change but itself is unmanifest and immutable. Thus *Bhāgavat's* true nature is indistinguishable from that of *Brahman* alluded to in the *Upanishads*.

> Therefore at all times remember me and fight. When thy mind and understanding are set on me, to me alone shalt thou come without doubt. (VIII-7)

"Remember me and fight" (*mam anusmara yuddha ca*). This one phrase captures the essence of the teaching of the *Gita*. Faced with doubt and harshness of life, remember God and fight the forces of darkness and lower life. Combine *bhakti* (and *jñāna*) with *karma* and struggle on within your *svā-dharma*. *Anusmara* is a derivative of *smarna*, a synonym of bhakti. One must perform *karma* and be active by letting bhakti provide the sparks of energy and direction, consistent with the supreme goal, the ultimate Being. Only those are capable of realizing and ultimately merging with God (*jñāna* and *moksha*) whose mind and intellect (*mano-buddhi*) are dedicated to *Bhāgavat*; whose deeds are done in the shade of bhakti and are geared toward *jñāna*. At every step of the way, the *Gita* calls for a fusion of *karma*, *bhakti* and *jñāna* in an ideal and authentic human life.

"This is the supreme person (*Puruṣa*) . . . who can be gained by unswerving devotion" (VIII-22). One-pointed devotion (*ananyāya bhaktya*) is a sure means to attain what the ancients called *puruṣa* and was later called *Brahman*. The *Gita* does not distinguish between *puruṣa, Brahman,* and the *Bhāgavat.* Bhakti is a path toward it which is as certain of success as the path of *jñāna*.

> Whoever offers to me with devotion a leaf, a flower, a fruit, or water, that offering of love, of the pure of heart, I accept. (IX-26)
>
> For those who take refuge in me, O Pārtha (Arjuna) though they are lowly born, women, *Vaisyas* as well as *sūdras*, they also attain to the highest goal. (IX-32)

The offerings of bhakti (*bhakti-upahārtam*), the gifts of love are most valuable to the *Bhāgavat*. It is not the size or the cost of the gift, but it is the sentiment of giving that is important. Offering and adoration, the urge to give are natural aspects bhakti or love, and thus quite valuable. The path of bhakti is not elitist; it is open to all. Not just *Brahmins* (priests) but people from other *varṇas* (castes), even those from the lowest caste (*sūdras*) can do bhakti. Men and women alike can practice bhakti, can follow the path of bhakti toward realization (*jñāna*) of God and toward salvation (*moksa*).

> To those who are constantly devoted and worship me with love, I grant the concentration of understanding by which they come unto me. (X-10)

The ever-devoted ones, who worship (*bhajatam*) the *Bhāgavat* filled with love (*priti-purvākam*), to them, he grants a *yoga* of wisdom (*buddhi-yoga*) by which they can reach him or "realize him as their own self," as Sankara explains.[18] In other words, wisdom (*jñāna*) and bhakti, go hand in hand for the ever-devoted ones. Their love is rewarded with a superior knowledge that opens their eyes to a realization of *Brahman*. In other words, true *jñāna* is not possible without bhakti. Without bhakti knowledge is mere scholarship, it is not a realization of life or of God. Bhakti uplifts knowledge that is *avidya* (mundane learning) to the level of *vidya*, i.e., fundamental knowledge (*jñāna*). The exponents (*āchāryas*) of *Vedānta* schools, Sankara, Ramanuja, Madhva, Vallabha, and Nimbarka were all practitioners of bhakti as well as great scholars (*pandits*) who wrote copious commentaries on Vedic texts.

Arjuna wishes to see the imperishable Self of the *Bhāgavat*, after he has received instruction about the nature of reality and that of the *Bhāgavat*. After witnessing him in the human form of the guru, he wishes to see with his own eyes his universal form. The *Bhāgavat* accedes to his request. Arjuna has this marvelous spiritual experience due to *Bhāgavat's* grace. He revealed "his supreme and divine form" thus:

> Of many mouths and eyes, of many visions of marvel, of many divine ornaments, of many divine uplifted weapons. (XI-10)
>
> There Pandava beheld the whole universe, with its manifold divisions gathered together in one, in the body of the God of gods (*devadevasya*). (XI-13)
>
> Then he, the winner of wealth (Arjuna) struck with amazement, his hair standing on end, bowed down his head to the Lord, with hands folding (in salutation), said. (XI-14)

This dramatic interlude indicative of the conviction that *Brahman* abides in all nooks and corners of the world and all entities of the universe is shown as a reward for Arjuna's bhakti. Arjuna gets to see with his eyes, in fast motion, the processes of the reincarnation of beings doomed to repeated rebirths in *samsāra*. Arjuna pays obeisance and expresses his expectations of bhakti which are the same as the standard expectations of love:

> Therefore bowing down and prostrating my body before thee, Adorable Lord, I seek thy grace. Thou O God, shouldst bear with me as a father to his son, as a friend to his friend, as a lover to his beloved. (XI-44)

This passage shows that the ancient Vedic sense of bhakti as personal love is alive and well in the *Gita*. The new theistic understanding bhakti does not wish to lose sight of its rootedness in love and love's usual expectations. Bhakti is just an attitude, not a new religion, as some interpreters would have us believe. Bhakti however has a role to play for the innocent masses who do not happen to be *Brahmins* (priests) or pundits of Sanskrit, for those who are not well-versed in *Vedas* and *Upanishads*. Those who realize *nirguṇa Brahman* are the chosen few.

> The difficulty of those whose thoughts are set on the unmanifested are greater, for the goal of the unmanifested is hard to reach by the embodied beings. (XII-5)
>
> But those, who laying all their actions on me, intent on me, worship, meditating on me, with unswerving devotion. (XII-6)
>
> Those whose thoughts are set on me, I straightway deliver from the ocean of death-bound existence, O Pārtha (*Arjuna*). (XII-7)

Those who attempt *nirguṇa-bhakti* directly face greater difficulty, for to meditate on the unmanifest for an embodied person is a radical leap. But those who have reached the unmanifested, having become one with *Brahman* and having attained *jñāna* and are not in need of deliverance. But this *jñāna* of the unmanifest is an arduous task undertaken by a chosen few. For most people, progress to *jñāna* through *karma-yoga* combined with bhakti of the *Bhāgavat* is the pathway to salvation. "Those, who laying all their action on me" that is, the *karma-yogins*, who approach the *Bhāgavat* with single-minded (*ananyena*) meditation (*upāsate*) are delivered from the ocean of death-bound world-cycle (*mṛtyu-samsāra*). For most people the path of dedicating the fruit of action combined with bhakti of the *Bhāgavat* is more straightforward. In the *Gita*, the *nirguṇa* and the *saguṇa* are both combined in the figure of Kṛṣṇa, the *Bhāgavat*. Most commentators have posed a dichotomy between these two aspects of the supreme, on the basis of the passages such as XII-5, 6, 7 quoted above. In fact, Kṛṣṇa is both *saguṇa* and *nirguṇa* in the *Gita*. Krishna Sharma explains in her own way this multifaceted Being of the *Bhāgavat*.

> Thus it is not the absolute or *Brahman* which is personalized in the *Bhagavadgita*, as suggested by Radhakrishnan, Edgerton and many others, but it is the deified personality of Krishna which is raised to the status of *Brahman*. Krishna the manifest, describes his highest state as unmanifest (*avyakta*). Therefore the monotheism of the *Bhagavadgita* does not rest on the fully evolved idea of a personal God. It was the result of the identification of the deified hero Krishna with the impersonal *ātman* of the Upanishads.[19]

Thus it is the various stages of bhakti combined with the various stages of the divinity of the *Bhāgavat*, that show how the human entity is a form of the universal Being. Kṛṣṇa is at first a friend, then a guru, and finally *Bhāgavat* identified with *Brahman*. As we said before a guru (Kṛṣṇa) is not just God come hither (*avatāra*) but a (human) guru gone thither. The same way *Bhāgavat* is not *Brahman* come hither but Krsna gone thither into *Brahman*. *Karma-yoga* and bhakti are the pathway to joyful performance of *svā-dharma* leading up to salvation, according to the *Gita*.

BHAKTI AND THE *GITA*: CHAPTERS 13–18

Since one of the fundamental teaching of the *Gita* is concerning the *svā-dharma* or *karma-yoga*, the intellectual support for this project is provided by *jñāna-yoga*, which is the primary theme of the last six chapters of the text. For the disinterested performance of *svā-dharma*, it must be realized that body (that hankers after the fruit of *karma*) is not the end but a means. The *karma-yogi* needs to be convinced that the soul is all in all. Says the *Bhāgavat* to Arjuna:

> I will describe that which is to be known and by knowing which life eternal is gained. It is the supreme Brahman who is beginningless and who is said to be neither existent nor nonexistent. (XIII-12)
>
> With its hand and feet everywhere, with eyes, heads and faces on all sides, it dwells in the world, enveloping all. (XIII-13)

These passages read like those from the *Upanishads* and emphasize that the *yogin* must realize that the soul pervades everything everywhere and is more valuable than the body. Real knowledge is the knowledge of the soul, which must be suffused with bhakti to produce *karma-yoga*. In chapter 14, the three gūṇas (modes) are referred to as impediments for the life of the soul and the main aspects of *māyā* (illusory worldliness). Bhakti once again delivers one from the tyranny of the modes:

> The three modes (*gūṇas*) goodness (*sattva*), passion (*rājas*) and dullness (*tamas*) born of nature (*prakṛti*) bind down in the body O mighty-armed (Arjuna), the imperishable dweller in the body. (XIV-5).
>
> He who serves me with unfailing devotion of love (*bhakti-yogena*), rises above the three modes, he too is fit for becoming *Brahman*. (XIV-26)

The connection between true knowledge and bhakti, knowledge that is bound to lead to bhakti is stressed time and again in the *Gita*:

> He who, undeluded, thus knows me, the highest person (*purusottām*) is the knower of all and worships (*bhajati*) me with all his being, O Bharata (Arjuna). (XV-19)

After the threefold analysis of the *gūṇas* (modes), a twofold examination of divine (*daivim*) and demoniac (*asūrim*) nature within the human being leading up to two types of human beings is undertaken in chapter 16. The following are but brief examples of detailed pen-portraits of the evil and the good.

> The demoniac do not know about the way of action or the way of renunciation. . . . They say the world is without a basis, without a Lord (*Isvaram*) . . . caused by desire, in short. (XVI-7, 8)
>
> The getaway of this hell (*naraka*) leading to the ruin of the soul is threefold lust, anger and greed (*kama, krodha tathā lobhas*). Therefore these three one should abandon. The man who is released from these . . . does what is good for his soul and then reaches the highest state. (XVI-21, 22)

Next, the three modes are applied to the various kinds of worshippers in chapter 17.

> Good men worship the gods, the passionate worship the demigods and demons and others, the dull, worship the spirits and ghosts. (XVII-4)

But the best worship is that of *Brahman*, it is implied by the final analysis of *Aum Tat Sat*, the symbol of *Brahman*. However, the lack of true faith (*sraddhā*), that is, without bhakti, all offerings, all penances, rites are false (*asat*), says the last passage of chapter 17.

In the last chapter, chapter 18, of the *Gita*, some concluding thoughts and a synopsis are given. "The wise understand by renunciation the giving up of works prompted by desire: the abandonment of the fruits" (XVIII-2). The renunciation of everything or total asceticism in the name of religion is not advised. "Verily renunciation of any duty that ought to be done is not right" (XVIII-7). The *Bhāgavat* expresses his profound statement "Remember me and fight" in other words by way of a summation of the *Gita* (XVIII-46):

> That from whom all beings arise and by whom all this is pervaded—by worshipping (*abhyarcya*) that through the performance of his own duty does man attain perfection (*siddhi*).

ENDNOTES

1. R. C. Zaehner, *The Bhagavadgita* (London: Oxford University Press, 1973), p. 7.
2. S. Radhakrishnan, *The Bhagavadgita* (New Delhi: Harper Collins, 1993), p. 14. All quotations of the passages are taken from this translation. Translations are sometimes slightly revised.
3. Ibid., p. 15.
4. Zaehner, p. 7.
5. Radhakrishnan, p. 11.
6. Zaehner, p. 6.
7. Dhavamony, M. *Love of God According to Saiva Siddhanta* (London: Oxford Univ. Press, 1977), pp. 11–44.
8. M. Hiriyanna, *Outlines of Indian Philosophy* (Delhi: Motilal Banarasidass Publishers, 1994), p. 117.
9. Zaehner, p. 4.
10. Krishna Sharma, *Bhakti and the Bhakti Movement* (New Delhi: Munshilal Manoharlal Publishers, 2002), p. 110. Works quoted by K. Sharma are: J. N. Farquhar, *An Outline of the Religious Literature of India* (London: Humphrey Milford, 1920); G. A. Grierson "Bhakti Marga," J. Hastings, ed. *Encyclopedia of Religion and Ethics*, Vol. II, (Edinburgh, U.K.; T. T. Clark, 1921); R. Garbe, "*Bhagavadgita*," Ibid.; F. Edgerton, *The Bhagavadgita* (Cambridge, Mass.: Harvard University Press, 1946).
11. Ibid., pp. 1–25.
12. Ibid., pp. 1–25.

13. R. G. Bhandarkar, *Vaisnavism, Saivism and Minor Religious Systems* (Strasbourg, Germany: K. J. Trubner, 1913), p. 54.
14. Ibid., p. 41.
15. Radhakrishnan, p. 29.
16. Bhave, Vinoba, *Talks on the Gita* (New York: MacMillan, 1960), p. 19.
17. Bhave, pp. 25, 31, 32.
18. Swami Gambhirananda, trans. *Bhagavadgita*: *With the Commentary of Sankracārya* (Calcutta: Advaita Ashrama, 2000), p. 406.
19. Sharma, p. 119.

4

Bhakti and Love: *Nārada Bhakti Sutra*

Love between persons and between worshippers and their gods were indiscriminately denoted by the term *bhaj,* the root word for bhakti in the ancient Vedic civilization of India. In the later ages, as the model of human love was rigorously applied to the relation between human being and the deity, bhakti came to denote a specific meaning, that is, religious love or devotion rather than love (*prema*) in general. This tendency of interpreting bhakti as religious devotion of man for God is especially highlighted in the *Bhagavadgita*. The practice of bhakti as an expression of devotion is equally present in Jainism and Buddhism. Since specific devotional connotations evolved out of the wider and original concept of *prema* (love), a study of the connection between bhakti and *prema* enables us to reckon with the mysteries and fundaments of love, which continue to remain enigmatic for our intellectual as well as mundane lives. For "what is love?" is a question which continues to be a basic riddle of human life.

Bhakti has been an all pervasive perennial concept in the philosophical and religious traditions of India. It is discussed and referred to in the ancient as well as the later texts of the *Vedas*. In the *Vedas* themselves the root word *bhaj* and the various synonyms of bhakti appear. At the same time, the attitude and practice of bhakti never ceased to be present in the Vedic period. However, it is in the *Bhagavadgita* that bhakti is thoroughly discussed and put forward as the crux of man's religious quest of union with God and of its desired union with *karma* (action) and *jñāna* (knowledge) is emphasized. Among the various texts that appear after the *Bhagavadgita* are to be included the religious histories called *Purānas*, the philosophical commentarial literature including the works by the masters (*āchāryas*) of the *Vedānta* system such as Sankara, Ramanuja, and Madhava as well as the wonderful contributions of the bhakti saints of the early southern and later northern bhakti movements. Within this voluminous literature are to be found some specific texts that explore philosophically the very nature of bhakti. Among the classical works in this class, which not only apply bhakti but theoretically expose its meaning, nature, potentials, and merits are to be included *Śāndhilya Bhakti Sutra* and *Nārada Bhakti Sutra*. Even though these texts focus on the theistic dimension of bhakti, nevertheless they trace bhakti back to its original ground of *prema*. The connection between bhakti and love is lucidly exposed in the *Nārada Bhakti Sutra* composed around 1000 A.D. by an unknown author. This text composed of eighty-four aphorisms seems to meet the expectation that philosophy should not merely explain reality but must explore possibilities of better living.

The pursuit of the meaning of *bhakti* in the texts such as *Nārada Bhakti Sutra* is bound to expose the nature and role of love in human existence. Although the *sutra* invokes the idea of higher love (*parama prema*) to expose the nature of bhakti as such, the text can also be approached to discover the peculiar answer given to the perennial question concerning the nature of love by the eastern tradition rooted in the Vedic heritage. The intertwining of bhakti and *prema* produced a peculiar concept of love that penetrates the philosophical, religious, cultural, literary, and aesthetic traditions of India in a far-reaching way. Thus, the measure of bhakti came to evaluate the standards of human and conceptual love as well as literary and artistic values in a fundamental way. Thus *Nārada Bhakti Sutra* is a text that elucidates the nature of devotional as well as secular love. It can be viewed as a treatise on the nature of love in general (as a *prema sutra*) and not just as an exposition of love between the devotee (*bhakta*) and the deity (*bhāgavan*).

The work asserts that *bhakti* is indeed of the nature of supreme love (*parama-prema-rūpa*). The *Nārada Bhakti Sutra* seems to invoke the essence of bhakti as understood and practiced in the *Rig Vedic* times, while at the same time, subscribing to the *Bhagavadgita's* theistic treatment of bhakti. Thus before we assess the philosophical insights of the *Nārada Bhakti Sutra* concerning the nature of love, a brief look at the *Rig Vedic* concept and a short history of the practice of bhakti will prepare us for a fuller appreciation of the nature of the Eastern concept of love as exposed in this remarkable treatise.

The earliest expressions of bhakti appeared in the history of Indian thought in the Vedas. It would be erroneous to trace the origins of bhakti in the *Bhagavadgita*, which is certainly a pioneering work in the theistic bhakti. Bhakti is certainly present in the hymns of *Rig Veda* not only as an attitude of love, devotion, friendship and reverence, but in the several usages of the word *bhaj*,[1] the root word of bhakti, and in the numerous usages of the synonyms of bhakti such as *nivedana, archanā, smarṇa, priti, sneha, anurāga, anurakti*, as well as in the all important companion concept of *sraddhā* (faith). If the term bhakti is indicative of an attitude of love, devotion, reverence, and homage, it is certainly present in the *Rig Vedic* hymns of communion with the divine beings. Adoration is expressed for, mercy is sought from, and power is recognized of numerous gods and goddesses. Some aspects of bhakti such as recognition of a god's grace, kindness, and involvement in human affairs, as well as self-surrendering prayer (*nivedana*), symbolic offering (*archanā*), and sweet recollection (*smaṛna*) are all present.[2] Feelings of wonder, grace, confession, and repentance can be gleaned from the hymns of the *Rig Veda*. The notion of *sraddhā* (faith) certainly characterizes these compositions and the term itself is used many times.[3]

What is most remarkable is that the supplicant in the hymns of the *Rig Veda* constantly addresses gods as father, mother, brother, relation, honored guest, etc., and invokes God's friendship (*sakhya*). This means that religious love was being measured by personal or secular love, that is, no distinction was made between *prema* and bhakti. The relation with the divine was one of love and love's usual expectations, experiences, and involvements. The divine beings were perceived as dwelling in the vicinity, not distant either from individuals or from their world. This is indicative of one of the chief roles of bhakti; it personalized the deity, makes the deity part and parcel of the human world.

Bhakti as an ethical and thoughtful attitude continues to be widely upheld in the *Upanishads* even though the term bhakti appears only in the last couplet of the *Śvetāśvatara-Upanishad*.[4] Lucid historical evidence informs us that bhakti as a practice was in vogue in the Bhāgavata and Pañcharātra cults, which predate the writing of the epics.[5] It seems that far from being an originator of the concept of bhakti, the *Bhagavadgita* merely transforms what we may call existential bhakti to a theistic bhakti without denying its existential role. We may also notice that bhakti is very much part and parcel of the religious ethos and comprehensive philosophical worldviews of the so-called heterodox traditions including the great traditions of Buddhism and Jainism.

The thesis that bhakti as an attitude and a practice is present in the age of the *Vedas* as well as clearly mentioned in the Vedic texts, albeit in the usages of its root word *bhaj* and of bhakti's numerous synonyms and companion concepts, is certainly controversial. Many scholars of religious studies and indology, basing their conclusions on linguistic and etymological analyses, consider bhakti as nonexistent in the pre-*Bhagavadgita* texts. They also find post-*Gita* theistic bhakti qualitatively different from the polytheistic devotions visible in the Vedic hymns and monistic ardor for Impersonal Being (*nirguṇa Brahman*) present in the *Upanishads*. Dhavamony, who applies the model of later Saivistic bhakti movement of South India to all bhakti remarks:

> The Rig Vedic worshipper is yet a god-seeker, a god-lover, a pious devotee, a friend of gods, god-praising. But this love of God is not at all the later Hindu

> bhakti, for various reasons. First, requests for temporal favours, however legitimate, are far too much in the foreground. Second, the gods are constantly addressed as "our father, mother, brother, relation." Hence, the love of the worshipper for his god is rather one of family affection.[6]

A strong distinction between theistic and Vedic bhakti made by some scholars, ignores the essential meaning of bhakti as love, human love that is essentially love between persons. This model of human love between persons was later deemed to be authentically applicable to love between the devotee (*bhakta*) and the monotheistic deity (*bhagavān*). The transforming relationship between Arjuna and Krsna in the *Bhagavadgita* is indicative of Vedic bhakti changing into theistic bhakti. Their friendship turns into the bond between man and God. There are other scholars who acknowledge that bhakti ranges over the entire history of Indian thought and penetrates all philosophical systems and religious worldviews of the tradition. Nicol Macnicol, R. G. Bhandarkar, and E. W. Hopkins, believe that loving devotion is already present in the *Rig Veda*, and the *Rig Vedic* times. Nicol Macnicol is able to identify the beginnings of theistic thought in *Vedas*. He says that: "If we place together into one pattern these patterns of many-hued intuition we may be able to realize how near they approach the theistic conceptions of today."[7] Jeanine Miller remarks in the introduction to her comprehensive study of bhakti and the *Rig Veda*:

> The *Vedas* are usually studied for their mythological, liturgical, sacrificial or even social and ethical content but not for their devotional side. . . . Any personal devotional outpouring . . . is usually either minimized or ignored altogether. . . . Bhakti in the RV is summed up in one sentence by M. DasGupta: "Bhakti involves an attitude hardly compatible with the Vedic and Brahmanic idea of worship and ritualism."[8]

The real problem lies in forgetting that love does not merely abide in the domain of religion. Bhakti as *prema* is nothing exclusively Vedic or Hindu. Bhakti is the way love has been interpreted and applied to philosophy, religion, and culture by the thought systems of India. Love and bhakti is something that reverberates in every human heart. R. Vyas remarks:

> When was bhakti born? The answer shall depend on . . . when did the human heart come into being? . . . Bhakti is as old as human being. It is not meant that highly developed concept of bhakti . . . was present in the primitive past of humanity. What is meant is that the basic element of bhakti (*sraddhā* or faith) is quite old.[9]

Personal love or *prema* is said to be the soul of bhakti by the *Nārada Bhakti Sutra* (*NBS*).[10] While maintaining its theistic standpoint this text reiterates the

Vedic notion of bhakti several centuries later and not only pinpoints the essence of bhakti but also contains an original reply to the age-old and ever unsettled question, namely "what is love?" Let us now briefly explore the nature of bhakti as described by the *NBS*. Within its eighty-four aphorisms (*sutras*) also lies buried an exposition of the nature of love, the criteria for its authenticity, and a description of the potentials of higher love. *NBS* is undeniably an elucidation of theistic bhakti. It was written in an age when theistic bhakti was firmly established within Hinduism and the term bhakti came to mean the devotional love between man and God (*bhakta* and *bhagavān*) or between the devotee and the Guru (*şişya* and the *Guru*). Thus the term bhakti was no longer being widely used for love between persons or for deeper adoration for one another or for love as such, as it was being used in the early Vedic times. Since the later bhakti was essentially an application of human love to religious love, as *prema* was transformed into *parama prema* (higher love). At the same time, bhakti became a measure or a criterion for the quality of love in general. What *NBS* does is to explore bhakti all the way back to its ancient meaning that is *prema,* and while elucidating theistic bhakti, it invokes Vedic bhakti as well. This text evaluates the connection between bhakti and *prema* as well as exposes the inner nature of *prema,* while it gives several pointers for the practice of bhakti and explains why traditional routines such as avoiding bad company, hymn singing (*kirtana*), and search for a spiritual master (*guru*) are essential for a devotee. Thus, among other themes, *NBS* describes the lasting contribution of bhakti saints to the lands blessed by their sojourn. Most remarkably, we find the all important theme of the nature of love as such discussed in this treatise. We will select the relevant passages (*sutras*) that describe the inner nature of love. But our selection does not seek to minimize the importance of other passages that describe the nature of theistic bhakti. The limits of space also oblige us to restrict the number of *sutras* to be discussed.

In the manner of the ancient *sutra* texts such as those of Badrayana and Jamini, *NBS* begins with the exclamation "now, therefore" (*athāto*) as the first *sutra* says "now, therefore, bhakti we shall expound" (1). This thought-provoking beginning with the words "now, therefore" is indicative of the great need to delve into this all important issue, namely, the nature of bhakti. The first *sutra* seems to open the exposition by a poetic assertion: "(since it is so vital to know bhakti) now, therefore, we shall expound it." The second *sutra* declares "which is indeed of the form of highest love (*parama-prema-rūpa*) toward that" (2). Most translators agree that "toward that" (*asmin*) means "toward God." Chinmayananda observes that the *sutrakāra* (the author of the *sutra*) deliberately chooses a neutral term to avoid sectarianism by refraining from calling the object of theistic bhakti, Kṛṣṇa, Rama, Shiva, etc.[11] If we leave the issue of the object of bhakti aside, there is no doubt, however, that the second *sutra* views bhakti "of the nature of highest love" (3). It means that bhakti is the supreme attainment of love and the nature (*rūpa*) bhakti and *prema* the same.

The third *sutra* fascinatingly conjoins "also of the nature of immortality" (*amṛta-svarūpa-ca*) (3). The text provides us with the insight that bhakti or the higher love is a crossover from the mortal, that is, mundane, day-to-day existence. Love is a partaking of or a version (*svarūpa*) of nector as the tedium and bitter facts of worldly life undergo a transformation. The ultimate urge in love is the urge for immortality, that is an escape from mortality or the bland ordinariness of *māyā* (illusory, worldly) existence. The drive in love is one that seeks and obtains an elevation from a lower, matter of course existence toward a higher, more fulfilling state. Moments of love let one abide in immortality. Love is therefore fundamentally of the nature of immortality. The fourth *sutra* adds: "Having found this, man become accomplished (*siddhā*), immortal (*amrta*), content (*tṛpta*)" (4). The text seems to maintain that this gain of higher love is a remarkable attainment. It makes one successful and accomplished (in any endeavor); that is, anything done with love promises highest success. Thus, the *Bhagavadgita* emphasizes that *karma* and *jñāna* be combined with (*yoga*) bhakti. One becomes immortal, for love opens the doors to immortality as one ceases to fear death and regards it as inferior to love having been blessed with faith (*sraddhā*) that accompanies love. Higher love yields to the lover a satisfaction incomparable to any other in mortal existence and leaves one remarkably content (*tṛpta*), saturated, and complete with bliss.

NBS defines the standards or measuring rods of true love which is indistinguishable from the highest bhakti. While it describes the seemingly perfect possibilities of love and bhakti, it does not mean that all cases of love attain true bhakti. The text does outline the concept of love in Vedic tradition, a concept that penetrates the evolution of religious thought within all four of the Indian religions, Hinduism, Buddhism, Jainism, and Sikhism. Bhakti also penetrates fine arts, music, literature and cultural ethos of the tradition.

The *sutrakāra* states further that "having attained this (*parama prema*) one craves nothing (*vanchati*), never grieves (*sochati*), never hates (*dveṣti*), never revels (*ramate*), never becomes zealous (*utsāhi*)" (5). In a state of true love, one does not crave for worldly objects, one does not lament the worldly setbacks and separations, does not participate in the projects of hate and revenge. One does not enjoy lustful indulgences or gloat over them and one does not become overzealous over anything. One is so absorbed in love that other emotions and satisfactions remain unfelt and pointless. The next *sutra* says "by knowing this, one becomes intoxicated (*mattah*), still (*stabdah*), and absorbed in the self (*ātmaramah*)" (6). By knowing true love, one enters a state of sweet intoxication, mixed with indifference to worldliness (*māyā*), one remains held back, still, quiet, and stunned (*stabdah*) in a state of abiding in one's soul.

"Being of the nature of renunciation (*nirodha-rūpatvāt*) it is not moved by craving (*kamāyamana*)" (7); "this renunciation is that of all secular and religious commerce" (8). What the *sutrakāra* means to say is that higher love is not a lustful love but one that finds both conventional worldly excitements and religious ritualism uninteresting. Love is said to be an intoxication and quietude (i.e., indifferent to mundane preoccupations) at the same time. It is a transformation of the tedious mundane life. Of course "to an extent worldly duties are to be performed and occupation of eating, drinking, etc., shall continue as long as the lease of the body's existence lasts" (14).

Among the various spiritual authorities quoted on the nature of bhakti, the words of Śāndilya who also authored a treatise on bhakti (*Śāndilya Bhakti Sutra*), are quite thought provoking. Bhakti is "not opposed to the blissful enjoyment in the soul (*ātman-rati*) (says) *Śāndilya*" (18). Thus higher love is the soul's best reward, a blissful abiding in one's own self, which is so different from reveling in things external, which necessarily hinders life of the soul. This and other definitions of bhakti given by well-known Seers ought to be followed says the author of *NBS*, and adds "Just as (love) of the *gopies* (cowmaids) of Vraja (*Yathā Vrajagopikānām*)" (21). Higher love is not a love of abstractions, but comparable to the human and yet world-renouncing love of the gopies for Lord Krsna. The legendary love affair of the gopies with Krsna represents a commingling of *prema* and bhakti, for the gopies were supposed to be fully aware of the divinity of their beloved Lord.

"Devoid of the knowledge of the greatness (*māhātmya-jñāna*) of the beloved, love is like that of a paramour" (22, 23) "which is characterized by the absence of happiness in the happiness given to another (*tat-sukha-sukhitvaṃ*) (24). In other words in real love, knowledge of how the beloved is, what his or her good qualities and preferences are, is a natural quest, as one begins to enjoy giving happiness rather than merely the received happiness. In higher love (*prema-bhakti*) the process of giving love becomes blissfully enjoyable, for the lover is a giver and not a mere pleasure-seeker. When receiving is the primary consideration, love becomes illicit like that of a paramour.

In the next few *sutras* (25–33) the superiority of bhakti over *karma* (action and *jñāna* (knowledge) is elucidated. The method of love, the path of love is straightforward and direct. It requires no aids, intermediaries (priesthood, scriptures, scholarship) and is open to all without regard to one's gender, race, caste, or class status. Bhakti is greater and higher than *karma* and *jñāna* due to "its reappearance as its result" (*phala-rūpatvāt*) (26). Among action, knowledge and love, only love is its own reward. Action and knowledge, often aim at something other than themselves, but only love aims at itself. Love wants basically (more) love. The path of bhakti is said to be superior "because of God's dislike for egoism and his love for meekness" (27). *NBS* gives the example of the royal household and a dinner to illustrate how bhakti or love works wonders and happens to be a method superior to action and knowledge to attain highest fulfillment of human life and/or salvation (31, 32). As *Sutra* 27 asserts, God as the ocean of love dislikes egoism and prefers the meek, who are neither haughty scholars, nor proud of their actions. Practitioners of action and knowledge often fall prey to egoism whereas the meek have only their love to offer and want only love in return.

All this is demonstrated in the example of a king's household which contains four classes: (1) counselors and courtiers, (2) military men and administrators, (3) the palace staff, and (4) petitioners and dependents from the general population of the state.[12] The king's true love is primarily bestowed upon the fourth class of dependents. Wise counselors and courtiers (representing *jñāna*) almost consider themselves the rival contenders and are quite haughty, and will fall short of a relationship of love with the king. Likewise the administrators, considering themselves indispensable governors of the state, will exploit their power and will fail to love the king. The palace servants who receive salary and are in the know of the king's secrets, will also not have a bond of love. The second and the third classes represent *karma*. Only the last class of people who consider the king as a loving father, depend on him, look up to him and regard all his gifts as blessings rather than remuneration will have true love for the king and the king will also have a tender loving concern for them. This example illustrates why the love for one's children is more intense than that for one's friends. Often the relationship with one's colleagues is loveless due to rivalry and professional jealousy. The need-based love between a man and a woman being one of mutual complementarity and dependence is often most intense. As *NBS* maintains "egoism" and "meekness," (i.e., openheartedness) make or break a relation of love. In the example of the dinner, it is not the activity of feeding oneself or the knowledge of the recipe and ingredients that is most important. What matters is whether it is lovingly served and lovingly partaken. Even a simple meal served by one's mother is most invigorating for this reason.

NBS thoughtfully exclaims that "indescribable is the inner-nature of love" (*anirvacanīyam prema-svarūpam*) (51). The *sutra kāra* remarks that in the end love is unfathomable and undefinable, "comparable to taste (of good food) enjoyed by the dumb" (*mūka-āsvādana-vat*) (52). True love leaves one speechless, dumbfounded. "But it is found to manifest itself in some rare deserving recipients of it" (*prakāşyate-kva-api pātre*) (53). In other words, the only statements on love are the lives of those who have truly loved. By using the term *prema-svarūpam* rather than *bhakti-svarūpam* in 51, the author means to indicate that bhakti as higher love (*parama prema*) is indescribable because love itself is indescribable. It is a perennial philosophical enigma, an ongoing amazement for the human entity. No individual treatise can exhaust its mystery. Love is not in need of proofs. "Because of the absence of the need of any other proof, it itself has the nature of a proof" (*svayaṃ prāmaṇatvāt*) (59). Love is its own attestation. It shines forth in the lives of those who have authentically pursued it and deservingly found it. Those who possess it do not have to prove it. It shows in their lives.

NBS confirms that bhakti essentially is an elevation of personal love, that is, it is not a different kind of love. Bhakti is an application of love between persons to the love between the devotee and God. The rewards of bhakti are well-known rewards of *prema*. The work expounds the Indian concept of love based on an overcoming of egoism and practice of devotion. The narrower confines of one's egoism are ceded in a realization of higher self (*ātman*) of its own accord in the process of love. "That thou art" (*tat twam asi*) is realized spontaneously as one's loving bond with all that it reflects in one's loving bond with someone. In the Eastern concept of love, bhakti establishes the standards of authentic love. The mysterious pathways of love are trodden with the mentorship of bhakti.

ENDNOTES

1. *Rig Veda*, 1–156–3; 8–32–14; 9–113–14; 9–113–2, 3; 10–151–2, 3, 7.
2. *Rig Veda*, 5–51–15; 10–151–5; 8–92–19; 8–102–15.
3. *Rig Veda*, 8–32–14; 9–113–2; 9–113–4; 10–151–2, 3, 7; See K. L. Sheshagiri Rao, *The Concept of Śraddhā* (Patiala, India: Roy Publishers, 1971).
4. *Śvetāśvatara Upanishad*, 6–23.
5. R. G. Bhandarkar, *Vaisnavism, Saivism and Minor Religious Systems* (Strasbourg, Germany: Karl J. Trubner, 1913), pp. 11, 55.
6. M. Dhavamony, *Love of God According to Saiva Siddhanta* (London: Oxford University Press, 1971), p. 55.
7. Nicol Macnicol, *Indian Theism* (Delhi: Munshilal Manoharlal, 1915), p. 9.
8. Jeanine Miller, "Bhakti and the Rig Veda," in K. Werner, ed. *Love Divine: Studies in "Bhakti" and Devotional Mysticism* (Richmond, Surrey: Curzon Press, 1993), p. 1.
9. Ramnarayan Vyas, *The Bhagvata Bhakti Cult and Three Avaita Acaryas* (Delhi: Nag Publishers, 1977), p. 2.
10. Swami Chinmayananda, *Love Divine: Nārada Bhakti Sūtra* (Madras: Chinmaya Publication Trust, 1970). This source will be used for the original texts of the

sūtras. All translations are the author's own and not those of Swami Chinmayananda. An earlier translation with commentary appeared in *Sacred Books of the Hindus* series (Vol. 7, 1918) for a reprint of which, see Nandalal Sinha, *Bhaktisūtras of Nārada* (Delhi: Munshiram Manoharlal, 1998). Both Sinha and Chinmayanada translations introduce highly theistic interpolations into the translated text, the former doing more so than the latter. Thus, both these translations are neither faithful nor exact. The commentaries of Chinmayananda are quite lucid and helpful, however.

11. Swami Chinmayananda, *Love Divine*, p. 3.

12. Nandalal Sinha, *Bhakti Sutras of Narada* (Delhi: Munshilal Manoharlas, 1998), pp. 15–16.

5

Bhakti and the Philosophies of Art

Is art an original description of the human world or an original expression of higher love? In the Eastern traditions, the depiction of the life of higher love has been one of the foremost aims of art. Bhakti is not only the expressed purpose of a sublime artwork in the Vedic heritage, but also serves as a measure of the being of an artwork. An artwork is not only a by-product of the act of bhakti but also an unfolding of the nature of higher love and higher life. Nevertheless, the phenomenon of bhakti is much misunderstood and often defined in the narrower sense of religious devotion. The narrower understanding of bhakti based on a limited historical perspective of the latest devotional movement within Hinduism has given rise to superficial philosophical problems concerning the connection between bhakti and aesthetics. One of these problems has to do with the inquiries such as whether bhakti is to be added on to the classical list of eight sentiments (*rasās*) given by Bharata in his *Nātyasāstra*, a treatise on dramaturgy believed to have been composed around 100 A.D.[1] Only a proper and larger historical inquiry into the meaning of bhakti will enable us to understand the deeper connection between bhakti and aesthetics in the Vedic tradition. We shall see that bhakti penetrates art in a fundamental way and to describe it as one of the many sentiments (*rasās*) is to belittle the impact of bhakti as a pivotal concept of the Eastern heritage.

"Love cannot be described exactly, just as the mute are unable to describe the taste of delightful food," says *Nārada Bhakti Sutra*.[2] In the Vedic heritage the ideal form of love has been named bhakti, its literary root being *bhaj* meaning commitment, sharing, serving, etc. Bhakti is more properly described as a higher and purer form of *prema* or human love of all kinds. Bhakti was identified as an essential ingredient of all *prema* and *prema* was meant to be realized through bhakti. In other words, the dichotomy between the secular and the spiritual is overcome when bhakti and love are taken as two sides of the same coin. Although bhakti is clearly a universal existential tendency and by no means confined to the Eastern or Indian tradition, its four thousand years long history under the spell of the *Vedas*, nourished by Buddhism and Jainism is a fascinating lesson in the study of human nature.

Bhakti as a form of love, often understood as divine love is well known to the students of Indian philosophies, religions, and cultures. However, less known is the impact that the tradition of bhakti has had on the evolution of the Eastern understanding of love in general. This concept of love has moved the Eastern mind for four thousand years of its known history and is present in the classical literature of Sanskrit, Ṭamil, and other major languages of India. Thus, although bhakti is often recognized as a form of *prema*, it has seldom been recognized as the essence of the Eastern concept of *prema*. Bhakti is not merely divine love but the soul of all love, religious as well as secular and thus the soul of all enterprises of love including the various art forms. The history of the Vedic bhakti tradition reveals that love is supposed to truly become itself when it attains the level of bhakti. This history reveals the peculiar features of the Eastern attitudes toward love and point toward the fundamental needs, wants, and goals of all human love.

In the Indian tradition, bhakti has always facilitated a fusion between the secular and the religious. The method of personal love is planted into the religious devotion carrying the original Vedic meaning of bhakti as love between persons. At the same time the idea of religious devotion is carried back to define the ideal personal love. In this way, bhakti becomes the measuring rod of the authenticity of any and every instance of *prema*. This is most visible in the aesthetic form of literature as well as in other fields of art such as sculpture, painting, music, and dance.

The various aspects of bhakti are expounded with remarkable creativity in the two epics *Rāmāyana* and *Mahābhārta*. The heroes of these epics, Rama and Kṛṣṇa assumed divine status and are considered the incarnations of God and their names are deemed as synonyms of God. Thus Rama and Kṛṣṇa became the supreme objects of theistic bhakti. Mystics of the bhakti movements, well-known poets, writers, dancers, musicians, painters, and sculptors enacted and retold the episodes, the scenes, the events and the philosophies contained in these epics over the centuries. Since the epics narrate the lives, personalities, achievements, and interactions of authentic characters, the term bhakti is given much wider usage: reverence for elders and gurus, affection between family members, love between husband and wife, and for love between friends. In the *Rāmāyana,* Rama advises his brother Laxmana at the moment of his departure to his exile that Laxmana must stay back and serve the elders of the family. This way Laxmana can show his bhakti toward Rama (*bhaktibhāvisyati sudarsita*).[3]

THE BHAKTI MOVEMENT AND THE BHAKTI LITERATURE

The age-old concept of bhakti underwent a renewal in the so-called bhakti movements in the south beginning in the seventh century and in the North from the thirteenth century. It must be cautioned that the thirteenth century represents merely the fruition of the bhakti movement and not its actual beginning. The first eruptions of the movement are found in the passionate poetic compositions of the Nayanars and Alvars, written between the seventh and tenth centuries in the Tamil areas of South India. Spiritual life shifted from a polytheistic ritualism to a passionate and loving preoccupation with one God and his *avātaras* Rama and Kṛṣṇa. A sincere and emotional bond of bhakti became the ideal, as ritualism, scriptural scholarship, mediation by priesthood, and mortification of flesh in the name of religion were regarded as superficial and unnecessary. Love as bhakti became recognized as the soul of all religious quests. This period saw the growth of Indian vernaculars, as Sanskrit, the sacred language was no longer the choice of many creative minds.

The literatures of modern Indian languages were born as the offsprings of the concept of bhakti. The spiritual authority of the priestly caste of the *brahmins* and Pundits (theologians) was much reduced as bhakti saints (*bhaktas*) and gurus emerged in all (linguistic) regions of India. Their devout lives and poetic and musical compositions won the hearts of millions. The devotional religion showed that the bond with *Isvara* (God) required nothing but love and that the kindness of a living Lord knew no distinctions of gender, caste, or sectarianism. The path of loving bhakti offered a much needed support and strength to people weakened and disheartened by oppressive ruling classes composed of alien military adventurers and a corrupt priesthood, as well as by a rigid caste system. Bhakti offered dignity, strength, and joy of life to the masses in all parts of the subcontinent, as the lovers and bards of the almighty offered the gift of their invigorating love songs that showed the prospect of a fearless, meaningful, and devotional life in the midst of religious decadence, political chaos, and social unrest. Bhakti did not merely redefine the religious quest but became the measure of all that is valuable in human life, all that is highest in the creative life of letters, music, and art. In the words of J. T. F. Jordens:

> In the first centuries of their growth all modern Indian vernacular literatures were moulded by this religious movement, and thus were essentially mass literatures. . . . The brahmans lost much of their spiritual authority which passed to saints and the gurus whose songs and biographies soon became a new scripture.[4]

Major figures among the bhakti saints were Jñānesvara (1271–1296), Namdev (1270–1370), Eknath (1533–1599), Tukaram (1598–1650), and

Ramdas (1608–1681), all from Maharashtra who wrote in Marathi, the first modern Indian language whose classical literature was shaped by bhakti.[5] In Bengal, the bhakti movement was nourished by the sublime devotional works of Jayadeva (twelfth century), Chandidas (fourteenth century), Vidyapati (fifteenth century), and Chaitanya (1485–1533). From the northern largely Hindi-speaking regions came Ramananda (1400–1470), Kabir (1440–1518), Tulsidas (1532–1623), Mirabai (1503–1573), Surdas (1483–1563), some of the greatest soul makers of the Hindu faith. In Panjab appeared Nanak (1469–1539), one of the most original practitioners of the way of bhakti and founder of the new religion of Sikhism. Other modern languages such as Oriya, Assamese, Kashmiri, and Gujrati had their own bhakti poets who made their lasting mark on the hearts and souls of the people. In the southern states, in the Tamil-, Kannada-, Telugu-, and Malyalam-speaking areas numerous bhakti saints made their lasting contribution to the literatures and cultures of these lands. In the south the bhakti movement began in the seventh century with the divine folk literature of Nayanars and Alvars, a series of saint poets. Scholars differ on whether to treat the southern and northern movements as one or as two separate eruptions of bhakti.

Bhakti influenced all mystical and religious movements of foreign origin embraced by some sections of the Indian population. For instance, the literature of Sufism composed in Indian languages is definitely influenced by bhakti ideals. In the work of Bulle Shah, a seventeenth-century Punjabi Sufi Muslim poet, the bhakti ideals are cherished and there are several references to the Krishna figure. Bhakti as a measure of human love cuts across the religious and sectarian lines in Indian literatures.

The work of the bhakti saints in both north and south India is characterized by a very personal and passionate longing to identify with the object of devotion. Self-effacement and self-surrender remain the most valuable aspects of such devotion. Such self-effacement is visible in the following stanza of the seventeenth-century Marathi Bhakti saint Tukaram:

> My Self I've rendered up to thee
> I've cast it from me utterly
> Now here before the Lord I stand
> The Self within me now is dead
> And Thou enthroned in its stead
> Yes this, I, Tuka, testify
> No longer now is "me" or "my."[6]

Bhakti was understood as a higher love in which the subject–object dichotomy is transcended in a compelling self-surrender and the self is freed of all self-centeredness. Individuals who were innocent of scholarly reasoning and tired of ritualism were shown a path of love toward the *Ish* (beloved lord). Any elimination or even subjugation of human love was not required, only the redirection of it toward a more worthy object and an overcoming of self-centeredness were needed. Thus bhakti set up the standards of love and showed that a person's extension into the self of the beloved is the fundamental longing of all human love.

It is hard to tell in a few pages the story of the bhakti movement which revived and strengthened Hinduism when it was facing internal decay as well as external threats. The works of the numerous bhakti saints are so massive, so thoughtful, so deeply religious that no individual scholarly assessment can do justice to them. Two fundamental errors and sweeping presuppositions that assail almost all scholarly treatments of the so-called bhakti movement are that most of them operate on a limited notion of bhakti as the "theistic Hindu devotion." At the same time, most of the secondary works on Indian philosophy and religious studies have a tendency to turn a blind eye to the pluralistic nature of this body of literature. Not only that they take bhakti as indistinguishable from "theism," they also fail to distinguish between the original contributions of the various bhakti saints, some of whom founded new sects and even new religions. Thus they bring the religious, literary, artistic, and cultural innovations of the period under the umbrella of the bhakti movement. In fact, there were several distinct attempts to define the religious truth within the bhakti movement with their distinct achievements and their distinct repercussions. Krishna Sharma in her valuable book *Bhakti and the Bhakti Movement*, points out that:

> What is referred to as the Bhakti movement was not a unified homogenous movement as such. The designation, in fact, covers a number of religious movements—each with its own distinctive features and ethos. Some of them were even antithetical to one another, not withstanding their common denominator, bhakti.[7]

Krishna Sharma maintains that an erroneous and simplistic notion of bhakti was introduced by Western indologists of the nineteenth century that subsequently became the standard academic definition of bhakti. The ideas of these indologists were readily incorporated and used as a foundation by Indian scholars in the fields of history, religious studies, philosophy, and sociology with minor modifications. The theories of indologists like H. H. Wilson, Albrecht Weber, Lorinser, Monier-Williams, and Grierson became the standard accounts of bhakti which gave rise to a "monolithic" and homogenous account of the medieval bhakti movement. By and large these indologists used Western concepts of polytheism, monism, monotheism, or pantheism to explain Hindu religious beliefs and applied these categories to both ancient and medieval unfoldings of devotionalism within Hinduism. According to Krishna Sharma for the most part Vaishnava-bhakti was taken as bhakti religion as such and its intellectual foundations were traced in the theological treatises of the Vaisnava Vedānta āchāryas, Ramanuja, Nimbarka, Madhava, and Vallabha who were viewed as reacting to the *advaita* system of Sankara. Thus Sankara's thought about *nirguṇa* (attributeless) *brahman* was understood as having little or no bhakti in it whereas subsequent Vedānta masters like Ramanuja and Madhava were given the title of *bhakti-āchāryas* who will provide the theoretical foundations and inspiration to the various bhakti saints of the medieval bhakti movement.

Krishna Sharma finds all the presuppositions of the Western pioneers of indology and their Indian followers wrong with respect to their very basic definition of bhakti. She describes her own intellectual journey toward an authentic understanding of this perennial concept as follows:

> The given definition of bhakti seemed not only non-viable but also erroneous; similarly the monolithic approach to the Bhakti movement, as both unwarranted and untenable. . . . I was convinced of the necessity to review the existing terms of reference and of the need for a new perspective of the bhakti and the bhakti movement. . . .
>
> In all academic works, historical as well as others, bhakti is defined as monotheism based on devotion to a personal God and as the opposite pole of the monistic stream of Hindu religious tradition which advocates belief in an impersonal God. Bhakti is therefore understood as antithesis of *advaita Vedānta* and its emphasis on *jñāna*. What is known as Bhakti movement is interpreted in accordance with these specifications of bhakti.[8]

Thus, according to Krishna Sharma, some of the wrong assumptions of the nineteenth-century scholarship on bhakti were as follows: "(a) that bhakti was a religious mode and belief; (b) that Bhakti movement was an assertion of the 'Bhakti religion' against the path of *jñāna* and the *advaita* Vedānta; (c) that Bhakti movement had a unitary character. . . ; and (d) that the systems of Vedānta propounded by Ramanuja, Nimbarka, Madhava, and Vallabha constituted the ideological base of the Bhakti movement."[9] Thus Krishna Sharma challenges all these assumptions and rightly points out that there was no such thing as a bhakti religion, that is, adoption of the method of bhakti by a religious thinker should not de-emphasize that thinker's other religio-philosophical contributions. In other words, just because Kabir and Nanak follow their unique methods of bhakti does not mean that they reject and de-emphasize the quest of *jñāna*. The various bhakti saints were obviously the practitioners of the method of bhakti. But that fact neither makes their quest for bhakti, nor their quest for religious truth, selfsame. Krishna Sharma correctly points out that there is no common ideology among the bhakti saints, but then herself commits the error of dividing them into two broad categories: *saguna-bhaktas* and *nirguṇa-bhaktas*, that is, those who believe in a personal deity (worshipping Visnu or his incarnations Kṛṣṇa or Rama) as opposed to those who believe in an impersonal and attributeless God. In the latter category she identifies Kabir, Nanak, Dadu, and Ravidas, who stand closer to the advaita system of Sankara rather than the systems of Ramanuja, Nimbarka, Madhava, and Vallabha.

In our view, it is definitely a belittlement of the work of those bhakti masters and original seekers of religious truth to be placed in any such categories. Whereas their original explorations of truth and their authentic lives devoted to truth as they found it speak volumes about the pluralistic nature of Hinduism, the scholars of Hindusim have confused "pluralism" with "inclusivism." The idea of a unified bhakti movement, with bhakti being taken as "religious mode" or as an "ideology" rather than as intermingling of love (*prema*) with knowledge (*jñāna*), is nothing but a convenient oversimplification. Overlooking the fact that many bhakti saints had no use for the copious commentaries of the Vedānta doctors, the division between the theological standpoints of various Vedānta schools is used to create twin categories of *saguṇa-bhaktas* and *nirguṇa-bhaktas* by Krishna Sharma's account. She calls Nanak a *nirguṇa-bhakta*, closer in his concept of God to Sankara. But there is no evidence in Guru Nanak's writings that he was particularly impressed with Sankara's works, or that he borrowed any of Sankara's ideas through scriptural studies. Krishna Sharma, falling into the trap of Hindu all-inclusivism continues to call the new religion of Sikhism founded by Nanak a "sect," and Nanak, a "*nirguṇa-bhakta*," an interpretation that would be unacceptable to many scholars of Sikhism. Whereas it is true that Nanak's theism does not advocate worship of a personal God but a love-laden bhakti through the way of *nāma* (name) of God who is beyond attributes, it cannot be surmised that *saguṇa-bhakti* is altogether missing in Sikhism. That the *guru-şişya* (guru-disciple) relationship is central to Sikhism is evident in the etymology of the word "sikh" a modern version of the word *şişya* (disciple of the guru), and in various passages in the hymns of Nanak that emphasize the importance of the mediation of the Guru. How precisely a bhakti saint brings love and knowledge together in his thought probes cannot always be captured by the conceptual games of the scholars. Thus the originalities of the contributions of individual bhakti saints remain belittled or unacknowledged in most scholarly attempts to elucidate the theoretical foundations of the bhakti movement. At the same time bhakti itself is woefully ill-defined and misunderstood. That bhakti is neither a religion by itself nor a religious ideology is expressed thoughtfully by Krishna Sharma:

> Bhakti is a generic term meaning loving devotion or attachment. It signifies a feeling or a sentiment. . . . Its meaning gets particularized only when the entity

> toward which it is directed is specified. For example, guru-bhakti, Vishnu-bhakti, . . . Krishna-bhakti, etc.
>
> Bhakti is a general term, but it has acquired a specific definition and technical meaning in modern scholarship. The current theories about bhakti describe it as a religion and a cult, and also as a doctrine and a theology.
>
> The word bhakti is derived from *bhaj* by adding the suffix *ktin*. *Bhaj* can be used in any of the following meanings: to partake of, to engage in, to turn to, to pursue, to choose, to serve, to honour, to love, to adore. . . .
>
> Bhakti is a general and relative term which can be used in a wide range of contexts, secular as well as religious.[10]

The original lives and works of the bhakti saints were creative achievements of their authentic endeavors to make the knowledge of the divine and the real, indistinguishable from projects of love. In their original attempts to intermingle *jñāna* and *bhakti* they emphasized that philosophy and love must combine to create a joyful and authentic human existence.

BHAKTI AS A MEASURE OF LITERARY MERIT

Bhakti has been so dominant a view of love that it penetrated both religious and secular literatures, so much so that it became the standard of literary merit. Puran Singh says in his essay "An analysis of Panjabi Literature," that according to the Eastern standards,

> One does not produce real literature by the writing of books, nor can it be enriched by printing trivia concerning the debates and conflicts of daily life, or by the production of the tensions of the scattered and peripheral minds in the form of intellectual provocation, which is like making of lines over the water surface. . . . Real and pure literatures are the immortal words of the *māhatamās* (great souls). The nations in which such personages are born, receive the literary wealth in the form of blessed rain.[11]

Puran Singh emphasizes that in the East the highest literature is the bhakti literature, the lived accomplishments of prominent *bhaktas* whose work yields and praises the way of self-surrender. In his essay entitled "Poet's Heart" Puran Singh enunciates the role of the poet according to the Eastern measures of literature:

> If the visible world becomes the subject-matter of poetry it will be a pity. Every mind can describe what it is acquainted with. I am but man, woman, thief, friend, gambler, king, rich, poor. I can change the disguise and describe the experiences of any of these in an instance. What is difficult is to know a life higher than your own in the invisible realm, about which we wish to hear from a true poet.[12]

These remarks by one of the pioneers of modern Punjabi literature and an astute literary critic indicate that it is the presence of bhakti in a literary work that is the mark of its literary merit in accordance with the Eastern aesthetic values. To speak skillfully and impressively about the visible world out there is not as valuable as the exposition of the invisible but higher world. A superior literary work describes an ideal world composed of human spirit's higher possibilities, suggesting a fulfillment resembling immortality.

Bhakti and the love between lovers cannot be called the same thing but there is certainly a connection between them, as no form of love can be understood without reference to bhakti. In the Vedic tradition, the spiritual realization of love is always considered as rooted in the practice of bhakti. In the folk literatures of modern Indian languages there are to be found numerous epics, which narrate the stories of celebrated lovers. These Romeo–Juliet-type sagas, written in verse, are secular rather than religious in character but the ideals of love described therein approximate those of bhakti. For instance in the folk literature of Panjabi, one of the fifteen or so major languages of India, the histories of ideal lovers such as Heer-Ranjha, Sohni-Mahival, Mirza-Sahiba, Sassi-Punnu, inevitably end in a parting of the lovers at the hands of death. These couples realize love not through a physical union, but in the strength of their devotion to each other, measured by their readiness for self-sacrifice. An example of such legendary love is the story of Heer-Ranjha. There are over one hundred versions of the saga written by numerous celebrated poets. Some like Waris Shah emphasized that the boundary between secular and religious love was blurred in the case of Heer and Ranjha. No wonder that references are made to the legend even in the hymns of the Sikh gurus.

The attainments of the celebrated practitioners of bhakti, the saintly *bhaktas* have left a deep impact on the cultural ethos as well as on the standards of art, especially, the standards of literary merit. But the spirit of bhakti is much older than the so-called bhakti movement. It is the presence of bhakti in its fusion with *jñāna* (knowledge) that earns Indian philosophies the title of living philosophies. Bhakti began as personal love in the *Vedas*, transformed into religious devotion in the *Gita*, and ever since devotion continues to define and qualify all endeavors of love. Bhakti thus remains the measure of artistic merit of a work. Thinkers, artists, poets, and saints who embraced bhakti in their lives and in their work reveal the nature of human love. The love that was the object of their studies was not just a cultural phenomenon but one that reverberates in every human breast.

BHAKTI AND INDIAN THEORIES OF AESTHETICS

Since Indian philosophies trace a close connection between *jñāna* and bhakti, they earn the title of being living philosophies in the sense that they do not merely offer ways of thought but also ways of higher living. That kinship between the beautiful, the good, and the true was known to the ancient philosophers of India can be gleaned from the classical works of Vedānta and Buddhism. As Hiriyanna remarks in his pioneering book *Art Experience*:

> Not infrequently we find in Sanskrit philosophical works parallels drawn from art. . . . We have even more direct evidence in the numerous works in Sanskrit on poetics, which though their set purpose is only to elucidate the principles exemplified in poetry and drama yet furnish adequate data for constructing theories of fine arts in general. A consideration of the teachings of these works shows us that Indian aesthetics had its own history; and the process of its evolution . . . followed closely that of general philosophy. . . . (For instance) when the predominance of *rasā* came to be insisted upon as indispensable to artistic excellence, many of the systems of philosophy applied their own principles to its interpretation so that in the course of time there came to be more than one theory of *rasā*.[13]

Obviously, if the theories of art have followed closely the tenets of various philosophical systems and if the philosophical worldviews are themselves imbued with the value system of bhakti, then bhakti must have penetrated not only the theories of aesthetics but also the aesthetic endeavor as such. However, the obsessive preoccupation with notion of *rasā* (savor) in the evolution of Indian aesthetics masks the presence of bhakti within its theories that were developed through the application of the basic principles and concepts of the various philosophical systems. Nevertheless, bhakti makes its presence known, not as a supplement to the list of *rasās* but as part of the theoretical framework of aesthetic systems functioning within the various philosophical systems. For instance, as Hiriyanna elucidates, in the Vedantic theory of aesthetics the concept of *ānanda* (delight) plays a central role. According to Sankara networks of *kāmā* and *karma* (desires and activities) compose our common life. The suspension or removal of *kāmā* and *karma*, while their cause *avidya* (ignorance) continues, characterizes the aesthetic attitude. The removal of *avidya* as well produces the saintly attitude, according to Sankara. However the artist and the saint resemble each other insofar as both are engaged in disinterested and unselfish pursuits while they realize *ānanda*. When we are able to suspend the process of *avidya-kāmā-karma* and are able to transcend the "ego-centric predicament" of the mind, that state of detachment based on a suspension of the routine life yields *ānanda*, a gift received by the artist and the saint. Whereas the artist receives *ānanda* in sporadic contemplative periods, it is a way of life and part and parcel of the enlightenment of the saint.

This account of Vedantic aesthetics outlined by Sankara forecasts the aesthetic theory of Schopenhauer that describes the aesthetic experience as the suspension of ongoing tyranny of the will-to-live. *Bhakti* saints or a *mahātamās* "whose immortal words" are described as "the real and pure literature" by Puran Singh, serve as role models for the artists. For the life of bhakti was taken as truly artistic as well as spontaneously ethical one.

In fact the presence of bhakti in the Indian quest of art can be better witnessed by looking away from the plethora of the theories of *rasā* and the various theoretical accounts of the grounds of poetry and drama. It can be visualized in the fact that Indian idealistic heritage seeks a *yoga* of *karma,* bhakti and *jñāna* every step of the way. The purpose of art, the practice of bhakti, and the goal of *moksa* are intertwined with each other. The standards and pathways of bhakti serve as guidelines for the artists and the seekers of the spirit alike.

BHAKTI IS NOT JUST A *RASA*

Nātyasāstra, the legendary treatise on dramatic arts, as well as the other pioneers of the *rasā* theory who subsequently applied the notion of *rasā* to all forms of art, did not recognize bhakti as a *rasā*. Bhakti was never included in the list of basic *rasās*. Bharata the author of *Nātyasāstra* mentions eight *rasās*; namely exotic (*śṛangara*), comic (*hāsya*), pathetic (*karuṇā*), furious (*rudra*), heroic (*vīra*), terrible (*bhayanaka*), odious (*bibhatsa*), and marvelous (*adbhuta*). In the words of Hiriyanna,

> The term *rasā*, used in Sanskrit for aesthetic value, a term which literally means 'savour' or 'savouring' implies that art valuation is an active process of which delight is only (one) characteristic feature. . . . (Art) aims rather at inducting in us a unique attitude of mind which signifies not only pleasure but also complete disinterestedness and a sympathetic insight into the whole situation depicted by the artist.[14]

Subsequently, an early thinker on poetics Udbhata introduced *santa-rasa*. After some debate over the course of centuries, *sānta-rasā* (calmness) was finally accepted as an addition to the original eight *rasās* by Abhinavagupta who was an important exponent of Indian aesthetics. Bhakti and *prīti* were referred to as *bhāvas* (emotions) by Abhinavagupta and Dhananjaya, but they insisted on *rasās* being nine and nine only. Dandin and Bhanudatta also raised the issue of bhakti as a *rasā* but other theoreticians like Jagannatha strongly opposed the idea. In the words of Krishna Sharma,

> the controversy whether bhakti can be treated as a *rasa* or not has continued to this day. Even the modern scholars of the *rasā-siddhanta* (*rasa*-standpoint)

uphold divergent view in this regard. However, on the whole, the *rasā-siddhānta* recognizes only nine rasas. And these nine exclude bhakti.[15]

The idea of bhakti as a *rasa* was more rigorously followed by the scholars of Vaishnavism (Visnu-oriented) movement within Hinduism especially in Chaitanyaite or Gaudiya school of Vaishnavism. Among the Vaishnavite theologians, Rupa Goswami is best known for his authorship of *Bhakti Rasāmrita Sindhu*, a classical work on the nature of bhakti. Rupa Goswami strongly asserts that bhakti is a *rasā*, of course, from a Vaishnava standpoint. This line of thinking is followed by the advaita Vedānta scholar Madhusudana Sarasvati who wrote another bhakti classic titled *Bhagvad Bhakti Rasāyana*. Rupa Goswami tries to establish bhakti as a pivotal *rasā*, in which all the other *rasās* are embedded. Thus he describes twelve forms of bhakti-*rasās*, inclusive of nine classical *rasas* and three new *rasās* identified by him. Instead of calling them *santā-rasā, vira-rasā, karuṇā-rasā,* etc., he names them *sānta-bhakti-rasā, vira-bhakti-rasā, karuṇā-bhakti-rasā,* etc. *Priti*, *vatsala* and *prayan* are the three new *rasās* mentioned by him. Thus bhakti is not just one among many *rasās*, but the fundamental *rasa*, other *rasās* being merely its forms, for Rupa Goswami. Perhaps Rupa realized that there can be no experience of art or beauty without an experience of love. Bhakti penetrates all forms and experiences of creativity. Rupa also freely adopts the model of love between man and woman to describe the love between the devotee and Krishna. *Rati* (pleasure) which was classically identified as a *sthai-bhava* (abiding emotion) of *sringāra-rasā* (exotic *rasā*) renamed *madhur-rasā* (sweet-*rasa*) by Rupa, are all secular terms related to love between man and woman, which are pressed into service to describe the devotee's attachment to Krishna. Thus the original meaning of bhakti as *parama prema* (higher love) mentioned in the *Nārada Bhakti Sutra* is very much embraced by Rupa Goswami. In the words of the historian Krishna Sharma:

> Whatever was said by Rupa Goswami and other Gaudia theologians about the Bhakti-*rasa* had only one purpose. It was to strengthen the Gaudia-Vaishnava cult of intense love for the personal deity Krishna. The question arises as to why they chose the *Rasā-siddhānta* . . . a secular thought-system and not a religio-philsophical doctrine to theorise. . . . Emotionalism was the most dominent characteristic of the Chaitayaite, a life cult of Krishna worship; and emotions per se constituted the very subject-matter of the *Rasā-siddhānta*.
>
> The concept of bhakti as a *rasā* is often put to use in modern academic works to support the current theory that bhakti denotes an emotional religion of love for a personal God. It is not surprising therefore to find citations in them from the writings of Rupa and Jiva Goswami.[16]

In other words, although the implications of personal love are firmly embedded in bhakti, it is not confined to the tradition of the worship of personal deities in various Hindu sectarian movements. Bhakti is also a companion-concept of *jñāna*, the tradition of the pursuit of "knowledge" of the impersonal Brahman, the absolute, the Being of beings. Bhakti penetrates the *nirguna* as well as the *saguṇa* traditions. As far as Hinduism goes, bhakti is not merely relevant for certain (theistic) brands of Hinduism. It pervades all of Hinduism. In the fields of art and art contemplation, a fuller role of bhakti is narrowed down and misunderstood when it is described merely as a *rasa*. Its role as a prime mover of art is missed in partial characterization as one of many *rasas*.

INTIMATIONS OF BHAKTI IN TAGORE'S AESTHETICS

Rabindranath Tagore (1861–1941) was not only an outstanding representative of the Indian heritage but also served as a bridge between east and west. Although he shied away from the title of a "philosopher" and called himself primarily a poet, his writings do contain treatments of various philosophical issues carried out in a unique and poetic style of his own. Being an artist of first rank and a man of letters, he was quite interested in aesthetics. Some scholars believe that modern Indian aesthetics begins with Tagore.[17] Not only do the ancient Indian conceptions of art and aesthetics peep through Tagore's essays on aesthetics but he was especially adept in showing the rootedness of the ideas of aesthetics in the perennial philosophical concepts of the Indian tradition, particularly Vedantic and Upanishadic concepts, such as *ātman, brahman, ānanda, māyā, līlā,* and bhakti. This Tagore did, not by mimicking the classical Vedānta systems or classical Indian aesthetic theories but by presenting his original aesthetic interpretations of the Upanishadic worldview from a contemporary cosmopolitan standpoint. Thus, his aesthetic and general philosophical analyses are remarkable not only for their simplicity and contemporary relevance but also for their jargon-free, poetic prose. Besides his deep contact with the *Upanishads*, Tagore was also influenced by the medieval *vaishnava* poetry, as well as Baul and Sufi saints. He had a full realization of the fact that in Indian tradition bhakti is as important as *jñāna* to realize the fuller potential of thought. He was especially drawn toward the bhakti poets Kabir and Tukaram and translated some couplets of Kabir in English.

Tagore not only lets the ancient Indian thought come alive in his work for a world audience but prepares Indian aesthetics to offer its concrete contribution to the body of a universal aesthetics. He was especially well equipped for this task due to his well-balanced self-education in the literatures and philosophies of the West. Tagore was also aware of the popular aesthetic theories and issues in contemporary Western aesthetics. Being a popular figure in the world of literature, Tagore had the privilege of having personal conversations concerning the problems of philosophy with some of the important thinkers of his age, namely Croce, Bergson, Einstein, Romain Rolland, Russell, Schweitzer, Dewey, Keyserling, and others.[18]

Tagore's ideas on art and art experience seem to be imbued with the spirit of Vedic worldview as well as the spirit of bhakti rooted in his primary being of a poet. The following account aims to outline Tagore's substantive contribution to aesthetics based on his remarkable ability to reinterpret some chief concepts of Indian philosophy and in making his aesthetic theories and concepts ready to take their place in a Universal aesthetics.

In his essay "What is Art?" Tagore remarks on the futility of seeking a definition of art. "Definition of a thing which has a life growth is really limiting one's vision to be able to see clearly. And clearness is not necessarily the only or the most important aspect of truth."[19] "Therefore I shall not define art" says Tagore "but question myself about the reason of its existence, and try to find out whether it owes its origin to some social purpose, or to the need of catering to our aesthetic enjoyment, or whether it has come out of some impulse of expression, which is an impulse of our being itself."[20] In this passage Tagore forecasts his intention to contemplate the reason of the being of art in terms of delight, expression, and personality, some of the chief concepts of his aesthetics. He would trace the relationship of art to Being as such and the Being of the human being rather than defining art as one of the many activities of the human entity.

Tagore traces the origin of art through a reference to the genesis of creation as posited by the classical Vedānta systems of Indian philosophy:

> Brahman is boundless in his superfluity which inevitably finds its expression in the eternal world process. Here we have the doctrine of the genesis of creation, and therefore the origin of art. Of all living creatures in the world, man has his vital and mental energy, vastly in excess of his need which urges him to work in various lines of creation for its own sake; like Brahman himself, he takes joy in productions that are unnecessary to him. . . . Art reveals man's wealth of life, which seeks its freedom in forms of perfection which are an end in themselves.[21]

The idea of *līlā* or divine play illustrative of the truth that *Brahman* created this world not due to a lack but as a sport is clearly behind Tagore's notion that "the living atmosphere of superfluity in man" is the one upon which art thrives. It is an aspect of the soul within man that due to an inner impulse he participates in art:

> This living atmosphere of superfluity in man is dominated by his imagination, as the earth's atmosphere by the light. It helps us to integrate desultory facts in a vision of harmony and then to translate it into our activities for the very joy of its perfection; it invokes in us the universal man who is the seer and doer of all times and all countries. The immediate consciousness of reality in its purest form, unobscured by the shadow of self-interest, irrespective of moral or utilitarian recommendation, gives us joy as does the self-revealing personality of our own.[22]

It may be noticed that Tagore is as fascinated with the word *līlā* as he is with the word *māyā*. The word *māyā* appears in his poems carrying different shades of meaning. The words *līla* and *kṛeeḍa* are also frequently used in his poems.[23]

The Vedānta worldview with its rich concepts of *brahman, ātman, līlā, ānanda,* and bhakti are all present in Tagore's contemporary exposition of the reason of being of art. His reference to the invocation by art of the universal man is particularly interesting. In pressing into service the age-old concepts of his tradition Tagore does not, however, mimic any of the classical *Vedānta* schools which as M. Hiriyanna points out had "applied their own fundamental principles to interpretations (of *rasā*) so that in the course of time, there came to be more than one theory of *rasā*."[24] Obviously instead of using the ready-made classical Indian theories of aesthetics Tagore offers his own contemporary aesthetic interpretations of the Upanishadic concepts, an interpretation which is meant for a world audience and partly written in English and translated into several European languages. He uses the simple term "personality" rather than a more religious and scholastic term *ātman* in order to enunciate the truth opened up by arts and the delight that it generates by intensifying a sense of unity indicative of the truth that the difference between "I am" and "Thou art" is superficial.

Tagore seems to be impressed with the fact that the ancient Vedic name of the highest God was *puruṣa* which literally means "the person." This ancient name came to be a synonym for *Brahman* and within the later theistic and bhakti traditions such as Sikhism in which *akāl puruṣa* or "deathless person" is a name of God. Tagore can be viewed as subscribing to the personal god (*ishvāra*) rather than *nirguṇa Brahman* without ceasing to have a high regard for Sankara's thought. The ideas of "personality" and "expression" which are the cornerstones of Tagore's aesthetics seem to be simple and modern versions of the classical Vedic notions.

> Limitation of the unlimited is personality: God is personal where he creates. He accepts the limits of his own law and the play goes on, which is this world whose reality is in its relation to the Person. Things are distinct not in their essence but in their appearance; in other words, in their relation to one to whom they appear. This is art, the truth of which is not in substance or logic, but in expression.[25]

The concept of personality is fully elucidated by Tagore in its relation to art activity in which the world's human or personal significance is fully realized. The stamp of personality is fixed on an abstract world:

> In the dim twilight of our insensitiveness a large part of our world remains to us like a procession of nomadic shadows. According to the stages of our consciousness we have more or less been able to identify ourselves with this world. . . . In art we express the delight of this unity by which the world is realized as humanly significant to us.[26]

The expression of personality is the true impetus behind art activity according to Tagore. Man never receives passively in his mind the appearance of things around him but adapts, transforms, and makes his own, the facts of this physical environment "through constant touches of his sentiments and imagination." Thus man by nature is an artist. But art happens when a human being intentionally expresses its personal reality. Tagore seems to say that art is an attempt to put on record or make permanent the artist's vision of what is real to him or her. It is a record of one's realization of the unity between "I am" and "thou art," a stamp of one's personality over the world. Tagore illustrates this as well as the connection between bhakti and art, by referring to the homage that a throng of Eastern artists paid to the Buddha:

> There come in history occasions when the consciousness of a large multitude becomes suddenly illumined with the recognition of a reality which rises far above the dull obviousness of daily happenings. Such an occasion there was when the voice of Buddha reached distant shores across physical impediments. Men in order to make this great human experience memorable, determined to do the impossible: they made rocks to speak, stones to sing, caves to remember; their cry of joy and hope took immortal forms along the hills and deserts, across barren solitudes and populous cities. Such heroic activity over the greater part of the eastern continents clearly answers the question: what is art? It is the response of man's creative soul to the call of the Real.[27]

In inaugurating the modern phase of Indian aesthetics, Tagore seems to have taken stock of the typical problems of the contemporary Western aesthetics and responded to them using the perennial concepts of the Indian heritage. He has done so by answering in a creative, original, simple, and poetic way to the age-old basic enigmas of aesthetics, such as: what is art?; what is the reason of being of art?; what is the relation between human nature and art activity?, etc. At the same time Tagore seems to have made a concrete contribution to universal aesthetics by adapting a style truly cosmopolitan consistent with his role as a transmitter of Eastern ideas to the West and by using a terminology with which the Western reader is quite conversant.

The contribution of Indian thought to Universal aesthetics does not come merely in the shape of classical theories of art and art forms such as the *rasa* theory of Bharta, the various other *rasa* theories, and theories of poetry, music, dance, etc. In fact, it is the unique message of Indian philosophies themselves, particularly Vedānta, Buddhism, Jainism, and other allied systems, which have served as reservoirs of aesthetic insight and provided material for the formulation of modern and contemporary theories of art both within and outside the purview of Indian thought. The theoretical frameworks of the systems themselves, their inner messages, and most notably their fundamental concepts provide endless resources for modern universal aesthetics. Modern Indian thinkers with a cosmopolitan outlook, the likes of Tagore and Sri Aurobindo, have shown us how the inner depths of Indian thought can rise to the challenge of resolving the enigmas of contemporary aesthetic inquiries. Both these thinkers freely use perennial concepts thematically as well as literally such as Bhakti, *līlā, ānanda, moksa,* etc., as they refrain from attempting to formulate new *rasā* theories.

In his exposition of "art experience" in his pioneering book with the same title, Hiriyanna reflects as follows:

> The aesthetic attitude stands higher than that of common everyday life, which is generally characterized by personal interests of one kind or another. . . . It is for this reason that Indian philosophers, especially the Vedāntins . . . compare the experience of art with that of the ideal state . . . as *moksa*. But the two experiences are only of the same order and not identical. . . . To begin with, art experience is transient. . . . Secondly, art may prove so seductive that (one) . . . may grow negligent of (one's) obligations to fellow-men. . . . Lastly, impersonal joy of art experience is induced artificially from outside whereas that of the ideal state springs naturally from within.[28]

We may notice here that the concept of *moksa* (salvation) along with a subsequent reference to *ānanda* (delight) have been evoked by Hiriyanna to explain art experience, which he attributes on the whole to Vedantin Indian philosophers.

The notion of bhakti is all important in the realm of art and arts. The attempts to infuse bhakti as one of the *sthayi-bhāvas* (abiding emotion) or as one of the *rasas* appearing frequently in *vaisnava* literature of the Hindu tradition, has been a misunderstanding of the role of bhakti in art. Hiriyanna correctly reflects that "Indian aesthetics has had its own history and the process of its own evolution . . . followed closely that of general philosophy.[29] If these systems themselves were imbued with bhakti, then bhakti must have penetrated not only the aesthetic theories but also the aesthetic endeavor as such. That bhakti incorporates all aesthetic endeavors in classical Indian art is a fact. However, the obsessive preoccupation with the notion of *rasā* masks the presence of bhakti as a driving force of art. Art is not merely a description of the peculiar manifestations of the human world. In the Eastern tradition, the outlining of the life of higher love has been one of the basic aims of art.

ENDNOTES

1. See N. P. Bhadura, "Bhakti as an Aesthetic Sentiment." *Journal of Indian Philosophy*, 16 (1988): 377–410.
2. Swami Chinmayananda, *Love-Divine: Nārada Bhakti Sūtra* (Madras: Chimmayananda Publications, 1970).
3. *Rāmāyana*, ed. Vasudeva Sharma (Bombay: P. Javaji, 1930), II–13–16.
4. J. T. F. Jordens, "Medieval Hindu Devotionalism," in A. L. Basham, ed. *A Cultural History of India* (Delhi: Oxford University Press, 1975), p. 266.
5. Ibid., p. 268.
6. *Psalms of Maratha Saints*, trans. Nichol Macnicol (New Delhi, 1915), p. 79.
7. Krishna Sharma, *Bhakti and the Bhakti Movement* (Delhi: Munshiram Manoharlal, 2002) p. 1.
8. Ibid., p. 4.
9. Ibid.
10. Ibid., pp. 5, 39, 40.
11. M. S. Randhawa, ed. *Puran Singh: Life and Works* (New Delhi: Sahitya Academy, 1971), p. 127.
12. Ibid., p. 36.
13. M. Hiriyanna, *Art Experience* (Mysore: Kavyalaya Publishers, 1954), pp. 2, 7.
14. Hiriyanna, p. 24.
15. Krishna Sharma, p. 287.
16. Krishna Sharma, p. 292–95.
17. S. K. Nandi, *Studies in Modern Indian Aesthetics* (Simla: Indian Institute of Advanced Study, 1975), p. ix.
18. V. S. Narvane, *Modern Indian Thought: A Philosophical Survey* (Bombay: Asia Publishing House, 1964), p. 120.
19. Rabindranath Tagore, *Angel of Surplus* (Calcutta: Visva Bharti, 1978), p. 29.
20. Ibid., p. 30.
21. Ibid., p. 8.
22. Ibid.
23. Narvane, p. 132.
24. Hiriyana, p. 7.
25. *Angel of Surplus*, p. 10.
26. Ibid., p. 22.
27. Ibid., p. 25.
28. Hiriyana, p. 27.
29. Ibid., pp. 2, 7.

Epilogue

Bhakti is a feature of human existence that has to do with human involvement with meaningful projects in the world. Besides being a devotional involvement, Bhakti expresses itself in human urge to belong to something meaningful and something higher. It is the practice of love that lends passion to action and knowledge. Bhakti's induction into religion has been acknowledged and studied in the books of the scholars of Indian thought. But the common ground between bhakti and philosophy has seldom been recognized. Bhakti broadens the possibilities of philosophy and brings it closer to life. Philosophy pays its debt to life through bhakti.

That bhakti is present and open for cultivation in human life in order to explore possibilities of higher love was recognized in the antiquity of the Vedic civilization. Bhakti is universal but the way it received due recognition and existential practice in the philosophies and religions of India, makes for an interesting and useful study. Such a study is suggestive of the connection between philosophy and devotion while it is bound to offer new perspectives on the history of bhakti within Indian thought systems.

Our study has endeavored to go beyond the narrower interpretations of bhakti as religious worship toward its larger existential and philosophical meanings, which, according to our research, were very remarkably explored throughout the history of the thought systems of India. Crucial to such a study of bhakti is to recognize its presence in the ancient age of the *Vedas*. We have shown that although the term bhakti was coined a bit later in the age of the epics, the root word *bhaj* along with several synonyms of bhakti were widely used in the books of the *Vedas*. Love of the divine beings was practiced as a dimension of human love as no sharp distinction was made between personal love and religious devotion. Love was showered on the gods and goddesses in a way that was no different from love between persons. At the same time, adoration of the spiritual masters of various persuasions had established a *guru-bhakti*, that is, a special regard for the teachers who led exemplary lives. The texts composed in that ancient age of the *Vedas* and *Upanishads* bear evidence of the practice of bhakti. In the age of the epics which follows the age of the *Vedas*, bhakti became more pronounced in the cults that worshipped specific deities. As a part of the epic *Mahābhārata*, the classic text *Bhagavadgita* was composed in which theistic dimensions of bhakti were exposed without jeopardizing bhakti's original ties with human and interpersonal love.

In and around the age of the epics, alongside the political and economic transformations of the society, emerged numerous heterodox sects that challenged the beliefs and practices of the central Vedic tradition. The dominance of the priestly classes (*brahmins*) along with their brand of religion was questioned, and numerous ascetic (*Śrmana*) bands of spiritual explorers came into being. It is interesting that *Śrmana* sects practiced bhakti and revealed its newer possibilities. Two of the *Śrmana* sects were later to become major religions, namely, Buddhism and Jainism. We have shown in this study that many heterodox sects embraced and practiced bhakti in their own ways and kept alive *guru-bhakti* as well as bhakti of the truth (*dharma*).

Regarding the question of bhakti in the *Bhagavadgita* the scholars of the nineteenth and twentieth century set into motion some theories of bhakti which we have challenged. The overly religious and theistic interpretations of the role of bhakti obscured its connections with human love and human existence. Some scholars paid too much attention to the Vaisnauite and Saivite bhakti (worship of gods Visnu and Siva and their *avatāras* or incarnations). Without doubt Vaisnauite and Saivite devotional traditions have had a long history within Hinduism, but these are neither the standard, nor the only classic bhakti practices. Impressed with the theistic pronouncements of the *Bhagavadgita* and historical evidence of the *Bhagavata* type cults, the indological scholars of the nineteenth century viewed the *Gita* as heralding a new bhakti religion, a devotional faith distinct from the so-called Brahmanism and its Vedānta philosophy of attributeless *Brahman* and *ātman.* Thus these scholars created an artificial dichotomy between devotional and nondevotional Hinduism as well as a dichotomy between bhakti religion and philosophical doctrines. Some scholars even presented bhakti as a doctrine in its own right, which they thought was elucidated in the works of Ramanuja, Madhava, and Nimbarka, and viewed their bhakti doctrine as basically opposed to the nontheistic philosophy of Sankara. These speculations are untenable because traditionally bhakti is a practice and not a doctrine. If it were deemed as a doctrine or a philosophy it should have been listed in the classical compendiums of philosophical schools and doctrines such as *Sarvadarsāna-samgraha* (anthology of all philosophies) of Madhava (fourteenth century) or *Sarvasiddhānta-samgraha* (anthology of all doctrines) by Sankara (eighth century). But there is no mention of bhakti as a philosophy or as a doctrine in these or any other ancient anthologies or histories of the Hindu tradition. Bhakti as an exclusive school, cult, or religion exits only in the books of indological scholars. Of course, they are right in identifying some bhakti movements and some sects which practice bhakti. But whether these movements account for the creation of a new bhakti religion remains highly debatable.

Our study has shown that most scholars tend to forget that bhakti is not an exclusively Hindu affair. Bhakti is present in all Indian religions, that is, certainly in Buddhism, Jainism, and Sikhism. It is also embraced by and developed in minor heterodox religious traditions. Many scholars who have written extensively about bhakti have nothing to say about bhakti in Buddhism and Jainism or about bhakti in the heterodox schools of Jatila, Ajivika, or Cārvāka. Some briefly mention bhakti of Guru Nanak, the founder of Sikhism, as part of their discussion of the bhakti movements of Hinduism. Many Hindu scholars have a tendency to bring not only Sikhism but also Buddhism and Jainism under the umbrella of Hinduism and to derecognize their distinct worldviews.

We have shown in some detail that bhakti is an important component of Buddhism. Bhakti for the Buddha as well as for the *dharma* and within the *Saṅgha* (the Buddhist order) was deemed and declared essential in early Buddhism. It is evident through a reading of the Pali canon that an ethos of bhakti was in place in the times of the Buddha. Our study of *Mahāparinibbāna Sutta*, shows that bhakti practices were fully in vogue in those times of political and economic upheaval when Buddhism came into Being.

Our book offers an original study of the *Nārada Bhakti Sutra* to explore the connection between bhakti and love (*prema*). This classic text not only probes the meaning, scope, and practices of bhakti but also sheds light on the ever-enigmatic issue of the nature of love. It shows that the Eastern concept of love has to do with bhakti, for bhakti is but *parama prema* (higher love). Thus bhakti is acknowledged as a measure of love.

We have also shown that bhakti has always been considered a measure of the merits of an artwork. It is certainly regarded as the measure of literary merit, for bhakti literatures of all Indian languages set the standards to be emulated by men and women of letters. The classical literatures of the vernacular languages were conceived in the cradle of bhakti as their output invariably coincided with the bhakti movements underway in their respective regions. It is unfortunate that the scholars of aesthetic theories failed to give due recognition to bhakti as the prime mover of the arts and literatures of India.

The various thought probes and lived-world practices of bhakti within Indian philosophies and religions show that philosophy must not be divorced from life and love. A *yoga* of philosophy and love must yield rewards of a contemplative life. Contemplative life is bound to be a life of devotion.

Bibliography

Bhadura, N. P. "Bhakti as an Aesthetic Sentiment" in *The Journal of Indian Philosophy*, 16 (1988).

Bhandarkar, R. G. *Vaisnavism, Saivism and Minor Religious Systems*. Strausbourg, Germany: K. J. Trubner, 1913.

Bhave, Vinoba. *Talks on the Gita*. New York: Macmillan, 1960.

Chinmayananda, Swami. *Love Divine: Nārada Bhakti Sūtra*. Madras: Chinmaya Publication Trust, 1970.

Dhavamony, M. *Love of God According to Saiva Siddhānta*. London: Oxford University Press, 1971.

Gambhirananda, Swami, trans. *Bhagvadgita: With the Commentary of Sankara-carya*. Calcutta: Advaita Ashrama, 2000.

Gokhale, B. G. "Bhakti in Early Buddhism" in *Tradition and Modernity in Bhakti Movement*, ed. J. Lele. Leiden: E. J. Brill, 1991.

Goyal, *A Religious History of India*, Vol. I. Meerut: Kusumanjali, 1984.

Hiriyanna, M. *Outlines of Indian Philosophy*. New Delhi: Motilal Banarsidas Publishers, 1994.

Hiriyanna, M. *Art Experience*. Mysore: Kavyalaya Publishers, 1954.

Hume, R. E. *The Thirteen Principal Upanishads*. London: Oxford University Press, 1921.

Jordens, J. T. F. "Medieval Hindu Devotionalism" in *A Cultural History of India*., ed. A. L. Basham. Delhi: Oxford University Press, 1975.

Kalupahana, David J. *Nagarjuna: The Philosophy of the Middle Way*. Albany, N.Y.: State University of New York Press, 1986.

Keay, John. *India: A History*. London: Folio Society, 2003.

Macnicol, Nicol. *Indian Theism*. New Delhi: Munshilal Manoharlal, 1915.

Macnicol, Nicol, trans., *Psalms of Maratha Saints*. New Delhi: Oxford University Press, 1915.

Miller, Jeanine. "Bhakti and the Rg Veda" in *Love Divine: Studies in Bhakti and Devotional Mysticism*, ed. K. Werner. Richmond, Surrey: Curzon Press, 1993.

Misra, Krsna. "Prabodha-Candrodaya," trans. J. Taylor in *A Sourcebook in Indian Philosophy*, ed. S. Radhakrishnan and C. A. Moore. Princeton, N.J.: Princeton University Press, 1957.

Müller, F. Max. *The Six Systems of Indian Philosophy*. New York: Longmans, 1928.

Murti, T. R. V. *The Central Philosophy of Buddhism*. London: Allen and Unwin, 1960.

Nandi, S. K. *Studies in Modern Indian Aesthetics*. Simla: Indian Institute of Advanced Study, 1975.

Narvane, V. S. *Modern Indian Thought: A Philosophical Survey*. Bombay: Asia Publishing House, 1964.

Radhakrishnan, S. *The Bhagvadgita*. New Delhi: Harper Collins, 1993.

Randhawa, M. S. *Puran Singh: Jivani te Kavita* (Puran Singh: Life and Works). New Delhi: Sahitya Academy, 1971.

Rhys Davids, T. W., trans. *Buddhist Suttas*. New York: Dover, 1969.

Sharma, Krishna. *Bhakti and the Bhakti Movement: A New Perspective*. New Delhi: Munshilal Manoharlal, 2002.

Sharma, Vasudeva, ed. *Ramayana*. Bombay: P. Javaji, 1930.

Sheshagiri Rao, K. L. *The Concept of Sraddhā*. Patiala: Roy Publishers, 1971.

Sinha, Nandlal. *Bhaktisūtras of Nārada*. New Delhi: Munshilal Manoharlal, 1998.

Tagore, Rabindranath. *Angel of Surplus*. Calcutta: Visva Bharti, 1978.

Talan, M. L. *Śvetāsvatāra Upanishad Sanuvād Sankarabhasya Sahit* (Śvetasvātāra Upanishad with the Commentary of Sankara). Gorakhpur: Gita Press, 1965.

Vajira, S. and Story, F., trans. *Last Days of the Buddha: The Mahāparinibbāna Sutta*. Kandy, Sri Lanka: Buddhist Publication Society, 1998.

Vyas, Ramnarayan. *The Bhagvata Bhakti Cult and Three Advaita Acaryas*. Delhi: Nag Publishers, 1977.

Warren, H. C. *Buddhism in Translations*. Cambridge, Mass.: Harvard University Press, 1915.

Zaehner, R. C. *The Bhagvadgita*. London: Oxford University Press, 1973.

Index

Abhinavagupta, 95

Āchāryas of Vedānta, 3, 15, 55, 57, 68, 75, 83n9, 90, 104, 105

Advaita Vedānta, 15, 54, 55, 90, 91, 94

aesthetics, 5, 85, 92–95, 105; universal aesthetics, 98, 100, 101; Indian theories of, 94–95, 95–97; of Tagore, 97–101

Ajivikas, 27, 28, 31, 36, 105

Alvars, 9, 15, 87, 88

Ambapali, 40, 41

anātman, anattā, 9, 25, 41, 42

Anguttara Nikāya, 25, 41

Anugita, 52

Āranayankas, 9, 27

arhat, 14, 29, 37, 39, 46

art, 85, 94; philosophies of, 85, 95–97, 97–102

āryasatyas, 14, 33

āstika, 28, 30

ātman, attā, 9, 11, 12, 25, 53, 63, 66, 70, 83, 97, 99

avatāra, 12, 57, 61, 65, 70, 87

Badrayana, 79

Bhagavān, Bhāgavat, 10, 12, 13, 18, 28, 29, 30, 31, 33, 37, 38, 39, 40, 46, 47, 54, 58, 59, 60, 61, 63, 64, 65, 66, 67, 68, 69, 70, 72, 75, 76, 78, 79

Bhagaavatas, 10, 14, 15, 27, 28, 56, 57, 58, 59, 60, 77

Bhāgavat Purāna, 15, 24, 59

Bhagavadgita, 2, 4, 12, 13, 18, 23, 24, 28, 51–72, 75, 76, 77, 78, 80, 104; textual origins and authorship, 51–55; and *Mahābhārata*, 52, 53; problems of textual interpretation of, 52, 55; and a general analysis of Bhakti, 55, 60; and a textual analysis of Bhakti, 60–72; and philosophy, 53, 54

bhaj, 1, 8, 12, 26, 71, 76, 92, 103

Bhaktas, 14, 18, 19, 64, 67, 75, 79, 87, 91, 92

Bhakti: synonyms of, 1, 4, 8, 9, 12, 16, 24, 26, 27, 40, 45, 56, 66, 67, 68, 70, 72, 76, 77, 78, 79, 80, 81, 83, 96, 104, 105; etymology of, 1, 8, 12, 23, 26, 77, 90, 91, 92, 96, 103; and contemporary India, 3, 18, 19, 58, 86, 97–102; existential role of, 1, 2, 3, 4, 5, 7, 8, 11, 15, 16, 17, 19, 29, 53, 66, 76, 79, 82, 83, 85, 86, 88, 103; universal nature of, 23, 24, 78, 97–102, 103, 106

Bhakti movements, 3, 4, 5, 15, 17–19, 56, 77, 87–92, 96, 97, 105
Bhakti saints, 3, 5, 17, 18, 19, 56, 87–91, 97
bhakti-yoga, 4, 24, 57, 62, 66, 67, 68, 75, 106
Bhandarkar, R. G., 8, 20n12, 48n8, 59, 72n13, 83n5
Bharata, 85, 95, 101
bhāvas, 95, 101
Bhave, Vinoba, 29, 61, 62
Bhikkhus, 25, 26, 31, 33, 34, 37, 38, 39, 40, 41, 42, 43, 44, 45, 47
Brhaspati Sutra, 31
Brhaspati, Vacaspati, 32
Brahdāranyaka Upanishad, 20n13
Brahman, 9, 10, 11, 12, 18, 24, 27, 53, 57, 58, 60, 62, 65, 66, 67, 68, 69, 70, 72, 77, 90, 98, 99, 104
Brāhmanas, 9, 27
Brahma Sutras, 51, 52, 59
Brahmins, 28, 35, 37, 38, 39, 40, 46, 48, 68, 69, 104
Buddha, 3, 10, 14, 24, 25, 26, 27–29, 30–34, 35–48, 58, 100; times of the, 27–30, 35–40; the daily habits of, 33; death of the, 41–48; the last sermons of the, 38–48; rival spiritual masters of, 46; the last words of, 47
Buddhaghosa, 39, 47
Buddhism, 2, 4, 8, 9, 13–15, 24, 25, 26, 27–34, 35–48, 51, 56, 75, 80, 86, 101, 104, 105; use of the term *dharma* in, 25, 26; the writing of the scriptures of, 43
Bulle Shah, 88

call of the Real, 100
Cārvāka, 28, 31–32, 36, 105
caste system, 14, 17, 18, 28, 38, 61, 62, 68, 81, 87, 104
Chaitanya, 88
Chandidas, 88
Chandyoga Upanishad, 59
Chinmayananda, Swami, 79, 83n10, 83n11, 102n2
Chunda, the metal-worker, 44
contemplative life, 3, 7, 8, 19, 28, 62, 83

Das Gupta, M., 78
deva, devatas, 8, 9, 26, 44, 54, 67, 69, 77, 78, 103
dharma, 14, 25–26, 29, 33, 34, 39, 41, 42, 43, 45, 46, 47, 61, 62, 64, 104; *dharma-ksetra*, 61, 63
Dhavamony, 2, 3, 5, 9, 10, 12, 18, 19nn1, 48nn4, 54, 72n7, 77, 83n6
Dīgha Nikāya, 27
dukkhā, 14, 19, 25, 33, 41, 42

Eknath, 18, 87
ethos of Bhakti, 4, 15, 18, 19, 27–29, 30–34, 36, 37, 38, 39, 45, 46, 47, 48, 105

Gaṇa-sanghas, 36
Gopāla-Kṛṣṇa, 59
Gokhale, B. G., 24, 48n2
Gopis, 16, 81
Goswami, Rupa, 96
Gūṇas, 13, 71, 72
Gurus, 8, 11, 12, 18, 28, 57, 69, 79, 87,105; Guru-bhakti, 11, 14, 27, 28, 29, 30, 31, 36; *Guru-şişya*, 28, 31, 54, 79

hetrodox sects of ancient India, 13, 14, 27, 28, 31, 32, 36, 46
Hinduism, 2, 3, 7, 9, 15, 23, 31, 52, 54, 56, 57, 58, 78, 79, 80, 85, 89, 90, 91, 97, 105
Hiriyana, M., 14, 24, 28, 54, 72n8, 94, 95, 99, 101, 102nn13
Hopkins, E. W., 8

Indologists, 2, 52, 53, 56, 89, 90, 104
Isvara, Is, 17, 18, 60, 66, 87, 89

Jainism, 2, 4, 10, 13, 14, 23, 25, 27, 28, 30, 31, 56, 77, 85, 105
Jamini, 79
Jatilas, 27, 30, 105
Jñāna, 1, 2, 7, 10, 11, 12, 13, 15, 16, 23, 33, 34, 55, 56, 57, 66, 67, 68, 70, 75, 81, 90, 91, 92, 95, 97; *Jñāna-yoga*, 64, 66, 70–72
Jñānesvara, 87
Jordens, J. T. F., 87, 102n4

Kabir, 88, 90, 91, 97
karma, 8, 10, 13, 16, 25, 28, 33, 55, 56, 57, 64, 66, 67, 68, 70, 75, 94, 95; *karma-yoga*, 55, 65, 60–66, 70, 71, 95
karuṇā, 33
Katha Upanishad, 11, 20n14, 63
Keay, John, 36, 38, 49n22
Kena Upanishad, 20n15
kirtana, 79
Kṛṣṇa, 10, 12, 15, 16, 17, 24, 30, 35, 40, 51, 52, 53, 57, 58, 59–60, 62, 63, 70, 78, 81, 86, 87, 91, 92, 96
Kṣtriyas, 28, 38

languages/vernaculars of India, 5, 17, 28, 43, 44, 54, 86, 87, 88, 105; literatures of the, 17, 19n1, 86, 87, 89, 92–95, 97, 98, 105
līlā, 97, 98, 99
love, 1, 2, 3, 4, 5, 7, 8, 9, 12, 15, 16, 17, 18, 19, 23, 27, 28, 40, 56, 64, 65, 69, 75, 76, 77, 78–83, 85, 86, 87, 88, 89, 91, 92, 96, 102, 103, 104, 105, 106

Macnicol, Nicol, 8, 20n9, 21n34, 24, 78, 83n7, 102n6
Madhava, 3, 15, 55, 57, 68, 75, 90, 104, 105
madhyamīka Buddhism, 29
Mahābhārata, 2, 9, 10, 51, 52, 53, 57, 58, 59, 60, 61, 86, 104
Mahāparinibbāna Sutta, 29, 35–48, 105
Mahavira, 3, 10, 14, 28, 36, 38, 58
Mahāyana, 4, 14, 24, 30
Majjhima Nikāya, 14, 29, 34
mamtā, 61
Mara, 42
Max Müller, F., 8
māyā, 66, 80, 97, 99
Miller, Jeanine, 78
Mirābai, 88
moha, 61, 66
moksa, 68, 95,101,
monotheism, 19, 53, 89, 90
Mulā-madhyamīka-kārikas, 29
Murty, T. R. V., 9

Nagarjuna, 29
nāma, 18, 19
Namdev, 87
Nanak, Guru, 18, 88, 90, 91, 105
Nārada Bhakti Sutra, 4, 15–17, 23, 24, 76, 79–83, 85, 105
Nāstikas, 23, 27, 30, 31
Nātyasāstra, 85, 95
Nayanars, 15, 88, 87
Nimbarka, 55, 57, 68, 90, 104

Pañcharātra, 9, 10, 27, 52, 59
Panini, 10, 60
Patanjali, 10, 60
personality, Tagore's concept of, 98, 99, 100
philosophy, 1, 2, 3, 4, 5, 7, 12, 14, 15, 19, 23, 24, 25, 27, 29, 30, 32, 33, 34, 35, 36, 42, 51, 53, 54, 56, 58, 61, 62, 75, 76, 77, 78, 83, 85, 86, 89, 92, 94, 97, 98, 103, 104, 105, 106
Plato, 25, 35, 46, 60; *Phaedo* by, 25, 35, 45, 46
Plotinus, 23
Prabodha-Candrodaya, 32
Prasthāna-traya, 51, 58
prema, 1, 4, 16, 17, 19, 28, 56, 75, 76, 77, 78, 79, 80, 81, 82, 83, 85, 105

parama prema, 16, 19, 23, 28, 76, 79, 80, 96, 105
priti, 26, 76, 95, 96
Purānas, 4, 15, 59, 75
puruṣa, 60, 68, 99

Radhakrishnan, S., 52, 53, 59, 65
Ramananda, 88
Ramanuja, 3, 15, 52, 55, 57, 68, 75, 90, 104
Rāmāyana, 2, 9, 58, 59, 86
Ramdas, 88
Ravidas, 91
religio-philosophical sects of ancient India, 36, 37, 38
Rhys Davids, T. W., 39, 43, 44, 49nn19,23
rasā and *rasa* theories, t, 85, 94, 95–97, 99, 101

Saguṇa-bhakti, 29, 42, 60, 70; *Saguṇa-bhaktas*, 91
Saivism, 9, 12, 57
Sāṁkhya, 51, 52, 62
Samsāra, 19, 29, 31, 69, 70
Samyutta Nikāya, 30
ŚāndilyaBhakti Sutra, 15, 24, 76
Sangha, 25, 32, 38, 42, 46
Sankara, 3, 15, 55, 57, 68, 75, 90, 94, 104, 105
Sarasvati, Madhusudana, 96
sarira, 45, 64
Sarvadarsāna-samgraha, 31, 104
Sarvasiddhānta-samgraha, 31, 105
Schopenhauer, Arthur, 94
Sharma, Krishna, 56, 57, 89, 90, 91, 95, 96
Sikhism, 18, 56, 88, 91, 99, 105
Singh, Puran, 92, 95
Socrates, 11, 23, 33, 44, 45, 46
sraddhā, 8, 12, 24, 65, 76, 77, 78, 80
Śrmanas, 27, 31, 36, 38, 42, 44, 46, 104
sthai-bhāvas, 96
sukara-maddava, 44
Sumangala-Vilasini, 33
Surdas, 88
svā-dharma, 4, 8, 61, 62, 63, 64, 65, 66
Svetāsvatāra Upanishad, 11, 12, 23, 28, 40, 77

Tagore, Rabindranath, 97–101
Tathāgata, 14, 29, 34, 42, 45
theism, 7, 9, 29, 52, 53, 54, 55, 57, 69, 77, 78, 79, 83n10, 89, 90, 91
Titthiyatirathkāra, 28
Tukaram, 87, 88, 97

upāsakas, 26, 45

Vaisnavism, 12, 52, 56, 57, 90, 96
Vallabha, 15, 55, 57, 68, 90
Vāsudeva, 10, 53, 57, 59, 60; Vāsudevism, 52, 57
Vedānta, 12, 15, 25, 51, 52, 53, 54, 55, 57, 75, 90, 91, 94, 98
vidya, 12, 62, 68
viṣva-rūpa, 57
Vyas, R., 78
yoga, 2, 3, 12, 51, 54, 55, 62, 64, 65, 66, 68, 70, 71, 80, 95, 106

Zehner, R. C., 52, 53, 55

About the Author

R. Raj Singh is Professor and Chair of Philosophy at Brock University in Ontario, Canada. He is author of *Death Contemplation* and *Schopenhauer*, and numerous articles on the philosophies of Heidegger, Schopenhauer, Gandhi, Vedānta, and Buddhism.